Living Wills and Enduring Powers of Attorney

Mark Fairweather & Rosy Border

London • Sydney • Portland, Oregon

Second edition first published in Great Britain 2004 by
Cavendish Publishing Limited, The Glass House,
Wharton Street, London WC1X 9PX, United Kingdom
Telephone: + 44 (0)20 7278 8000 Facsimile: + 44 (0)20 7278 8080
Email: info@cavendishpublishing.com
Website: www.cavendishpublishing.com

Published in the United States by Cavendish Publishing
c/o International Specialized Book Services,
5824 NE Hassalo Street, Portland,
Oregon 97213-3644, USA

Published in Australia by Cavendish Publishing (Australia) Pty Ltd
45 Beach Street, Coogee, NSW 2034, Australia
Email: info@cavendishpublishing.com.au
Website: www.cavendishpublishing.com.au

The first edition of this title was originally published by The Stationery Office

British Library Cataloguing in Publication Data
Fairweather, Mark
Living wills and enduring powers of attorney – 2nd ed – (Pocket lawyer)
1 Right to die – Law and legislation – Great Britain 2 Advance directives (Medical law) – Great Britain 3 Do-not-resuscitate orders – Law and legislation – Great Britain
I Title II Border, Rosy

344.4'104197
Library of Congress Cataloguing in Publication Data
Data available

ISBN 1-85941-856-2

1 3 5 7 9 10 8 6 4 2

Printed and bound in Great Britain

Contents

Are you reading the right book?

Please note: if you need advice on making your will, in the sense of arranging to distribute your estate after your death, please see *Wills and Estate Planning* in the *Pocket Lawyer* series.

Disclaimer

This book puts *you* in control. This is an excellent thing, but it also makes *you* responsible for using it properly. Few washing machine manufacturers will honour their guarantee if you don't follow their 'instructions for use'. In the same way, we are unable to accept liability for any loss arising from mistakes or misunderstandings on your part. So take time to read this book carefully.

Although this book points you in the right direction, reading one small book will not make you an expert, and there are times when you may need to take advice from professionals. This book is not a definitive statement of the law, although we believe it to be accurate as at November 2003.

The authors and publisher cannot accept liability for any advice or material that becomes obsolete due to subsequent changes in the law after publication, although every effort will be made to show any changes in the law that take place after the publication date on the companion website.

About the authors

Mark Fairweather is a practising solicitor and is one of the founding partners of the legal firm Fairweather Stephenson & Co. He has co-written 14 titles with Rosy Border, including five in Cavendish Publishing's *Pocket Lawyer* series. He has two children and lives in Suffolk.

Rosy Border, co-author of this title and series editor of the *Pocket Lawyer* series, has a first class honours degree in French and has worked in publishing, lecturing, journalism and the law. Rosy and her husband, John Rabson, live in rural Suffolk and have a grown up family. Rosy enjoys DIY, entertaining and retail therapy in French markets.

Acknowledgments

A glance at the 'Useful contacts' will show the many sources we dipped into while writing this book. Thank you, everybody. We would especially like to thank John Rabson, Chartered Engineer, for his IT support and refreshments.

statutory – laid down by law (statute) passed by Parliament, as opposed to 'judge-made' law (case law).

values statement – (in this context) a statement of a person's beliefs about human life and death, usually made in connection with a living will.

welfare attorney – in Scotland, a person you appoint, while you still have *mental capacity*, to make decisions about your *medical treatment* on your behalf if you become mentally incapable of making such decisions for yourself. This concept has no legal force in England and Wales (see also *advance delegation*, above).

Frequently asked questions (FAQs)

Are there any official guidelines on what I should say in a living will and how to say it?

No. A living will can be specific or general. For example, if you are making a living will when you already know that you are terminally ill, you may be able to make a far more precise decision about the stage at which you want medical treatment to be withheld than if you do not know what the future may hold.

Your living will could deal with where you want to be cared for – at home or in a particular nursing home or hospice, for example.

By contrast, your living will could simply make a **values statement** setting out your fundamental beliefs about life and death as a guide for others to decide. As well as the suggested draft Living Will in this book (see Chapter 6), several organisations offer their own living wills (see 'Useful contacts').

Are there official guidelines for doctors about how to treat patients who have made living wills?

Yes. Doctors *must* follow the British Medical Association (BMA) code of practice, which is set out in the BMA report, *Advance Statements About Medical Treatment* (see 'Useful contacts'). We discuss the circumstances in which **medical treatment** does and does not require consent in Chapter 1.

Is my living will binding upon 'conscientious objectors' – that is, people who have religious or moral objections to my request that I should not receive medical treatment?

Yes. A doctor who persists in treating you against your wishes may be guilty of assault. In *Advance Statements About Medical Treatment* the BMA says:

> Health professionals are entitled to have their personal moral beliefs respected and not to be pressurised to act contrary to those beliefs. But the

> 'sanctity of life' argument or other values must not be imposed upon those for whom they have or had no meaning.

Conscientious objectors are therefore expected to make their views clear when the patient first raises the matter and, if necessary, to pass the case to a colleague. Also, the BMA adds:

> In an emergency, if no other health professional is available there is a legal duty to comply with an appropriate and valid *advance refusal* [of treatment].

Our draft Living Will (see Chapter 6) follows BMA guidelines in asking doctors who are conscientious objectors to pass your case to a colleague more in sympathy with living wills.

Can my family overrule my living will?

No. But don't leave yourself open to challenge – for example, on the grounds that you lack **mental capacity** or the information to make a proper decision. If you foresee this sort of problem, get a certificate from your doctor (see sample certificate, p 52).

What are the religious considerations concerning living wills?

The consensus seems to be that while **euthanasia** and **physician assisted suicide** (see Buzzwords) would always be sinful, refusing treatment may be permissible.

The Church of England

Cautious acceptance:

> Doctors do not have an overriding obligation to prolong life by all available means ... Where formerly competent people have expressed their wishes about the way they would like to be treated, these should form an important consideration for doctors in determining how to proceed. **Advance directives** should not contain requests for action which is against the law, nor ask for the cessation of **artificial nutrition and hydration**. Care should be taken to establish that any advance directive was

> not made under duress. We would resist the legal enforcement of such directives since the medical conditions envisaged might be susceptible to new treatment, and medical judgments would have to be made about whether a person's condition was such as to require their advance directive to take effect.

[This quotation is from a much longer statement – see 'Useful contacts' for details of the Church's website.]

Buddhism

It is impossible to generalise, as there are over 500 different Buddhist groups, but some Buddhists advocate living wills. The Journal of Buddhist Ethics lists several works on the subject: jbe.gold.ac.uk.

Judaism

Cautious acceptance: 'The conclusion from the spirit of Jewish law is that while you may not do anything to hasten death, you may, under special circumstances of suffering and helplessness, allow death to come.'

Methodism

'We assert the right of every person to die in dignity without efforts to prolong terminal illness merely because the technology is available to do so.'

Catholicism

'When inevitable death is imminent, it is permitted in conscience to take the decision to refuse forms of treatment that would only secure precarious and burdensome prolongation of life.' (*The New Natural Death Handbook*, p 47; see Useful Contacts, p 112.)

Islam

Islam permits living wills. The Muslim Burial Council says: 'Due to advancing medical treatment Muslims should prepare a living will in case of sudden illness and admission into hospital for major surgery, or being in a coma when one is unable to speak.' Muslim living wills are special, however – in addition to refusing futile treatment, they say that medicines must not contain animal or alcoholic ingredients, the patient's body is to remain modestly covered at all times, and unnecessary post-mortems are not to be carried out.

Is a living will restricted to care in hospital?

No. It applies wherever care is given – in hospital, at home, in a nursing home or in a hospice.

I am old and in frail health. My children are anxious for me to make a living will now, to prevent my being a burden to them when I become terminally ill. What should I do?

You must make your own decision. If you feel that your children are pressurising you, take professional advice from your doctor or solicitor before you decide whether to make a **living will**. They will help you to make a decision that is right for you. Tell them that your children are putting you under pressure. If you believe that your children may not have your own best interests at heart, you may wish to make a statement that they should be excluded from decisions about your future medical treatment.

Bear in mind that a living will made under duress or under undue influence will not be valid.

In an extreme instance, your children might, if they really had their way, wish your doctor to deliberately terminate your life. A living will cannot be used for this purpose: it is not the same as a request for **euthanasia**. Both euthanasia and **physician assisted suicide** are illegal in Britain, as well as unethical.

Suppose that in my living will I ask for artificial nutrition and hydration to be withheld in certain circumstances. Will the doctors be able to overrule me?

No – because while 'the *offer* of **oral nutrition and hydration**' is part of **basic care, artificial nutrition and**

hydration are, in certain circumstances (so the courts say), forms of **medical treatment**, as opposed to basic care, and your refusal of medical treatment is legally binding on your doctors. If you look at the definition of **artificial nutrition and hydration** (see 'Buzzwords') again, you may agree with the judge in the 'Bland case' that the techniques involved *are* medical procedures. As someone in good health, you may find the various procedures for artificial nutrition and hydration repellent and want nothing to do with them. All the same, you might feel differently if you were dying of hunger and/or thirst because you could not swallow.

The BMA recognises that you may change your mind and so, for example, you can withdraw your advance refusal of artificial feeding – as long as you can communicate this to the medical team. Reassuringly, the BMA says 'Attention must be paid to the individual's verbal and *non-verbal* indications of his or her comfort needs', so great eloquence is not called for!

Would making a living will invalidate my life insurance policy?

No. The Association of British Insurers says: 'We believe it most unlikely that making a **living will** would have any implications for life insurance, as this would normally arise when a person's life is all but over.'

Would making a living will invalidate my health care insurance?

No. To be rather cynical, the odds are that they might even reduce your premiums!

Can young people under 18 make valid living wills?

No. Minors – young people under the age of 18 – do not have the same legal rights as adults. The courts have indicated that a refusal of treatment by a minor, even with **mental capacity**, can be overridden in law by parents, people with parental responsibility (such as guardians) or the High Court.

However, the Children Act 1989 stresses that the views of minors should be sought and taken into account in anything which concerns their welfare. The BMA endorses this, saying 'It is good practice for children and young people to be kept as fully informed as possible about their care and treatment ... Where appropriate, they should be encouraged to take decisions jointly with those with whom they have a close relationship, especially parents'.

My adult son has a mental disability. Can I make a living will on his behalf?

No. Under the law in England, Wales and Northern Ireland, nobody has the power to consent or to refuse medical care on another person's behalf. It is a myth that the next of kin can do this. They have no legal power – not even if they hold an **enduring power of attorney**. Similarly, an **advance delegation** may have persuasive force but will not be legally binding. You can, however, talk to the doctors and nurses in charge of your son's case and make your wishes known. It is good medical practice for doctors to consult people close to the patient to help them to understand what the patient would have wanted and you can be sure of a sympathetic hearing.

In Scotland, people over 16 years of age can appoint a **welfare attorney**. Even if you live in Scotland, however, in your son's case a welfare attorney would not be an option because welfare attorneys have to be appointed while the person has **mental capacity**.

My Dad is now blind, although he is still mentally alert and can still sign his name. Can he make a living will?

Yes, but a special form of words is needed to make his living will valid (see 'Alternative validations for someone unable to read and/or write', p 48).

I have heard about *advance delegations*. If I nominate someone to make medical decisions on my behalf if I lose my grip mentally, will this have any legal force?

It depends on where you live. In Scotland, the Adults with Incapacity (Scotland) Act 2000 allows you to appoint a **welfare attorney**, who is empowered to make decisions about medical treatment on your behalf if you are unable to do so (see 'Useful contacts').

In England, Wales and Northern Ireland, the idea of an *advance delegation* is not as yet supported by legislation. However, in April 2002 the Lord Chancellor's Department issued a consultation paper, *Making Decisions: Helping People Who Have Difficulty Deciding for Themselves* (www.dca.gov.uk/consult/family/decisionresp.pdf). In a House of Commons written answer of 11 March 2003, Rosie Winterton, Parliamentary Secretary in the Lord Chancellor's Department, stated that the Government had begun preparing a draft Mental Incapacity Bill. It seems that this might introduce the concept of a *welfare attorney* to English law. In the meantime, the views of anyone you nominate will usually, at least informally, be taken into account.

In the USA, an *advance delegation* is often known as a 'Durable Power of Attorney for Health Care' and is much more widely used than in the UK.

I am prepared to undergo any treatment which can prolong my life until my daughter can come from Australia to say goodbye. Can I put this in a living will?

A request like this is called an **advance consent**, and it is the opposite of a *refusal* of treatment. You have the right to ask, but the professionals have the right to refuse if what you ask is not in your best interests. Bear in mind that you may be asking for treatment which ends up being both futile and painful. The medical team may well pull out all the stops to keep you alive until your daughter can get to your bedside, but they are not legally bound to do so.

Suppose I am very ill, but the situation does not exactly correspond to the circumstances described in my Living Will – what will happen?

The medical team will still be guided by the spirit of your living will. They will also contact anyone you have named in your Living Will, as well as your GP, to try to clarify your wishes. If there is still any doubt about what you would have wished, the law requires them to use their 'best interests judgment'.

Would my living will be binding if I turned out to be pregnant in my final illness?

There is no definitive *legal* answer.

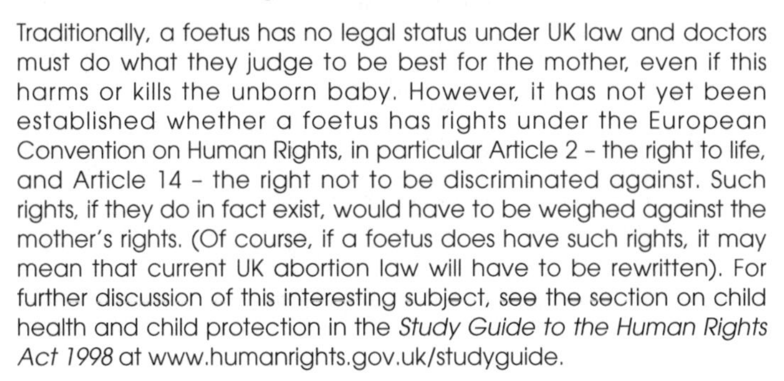

Traditionally, a foetus has no legal status under UK law and doctors must do what they judge to be best for the mother, even if this harms or kills the unborn baby. However, it has not yet been established whether a foetus has rights under the European Convention on Human Rights, in particular Article 2 – the right to life, and Article 14 – the right not to be discriminated against. Such rights, if they do in fact exist, would have to be weighed against the mother's rights. (Of course, if a foetus does have such rights, it may mean that current UK abortion law will have to be rewritten). For further discussion of this interesting subject, see the section on child health and child protection in the *Study Guide to the Human Rights Act 1998* at www.humanrights.gov.uk/studyguide.

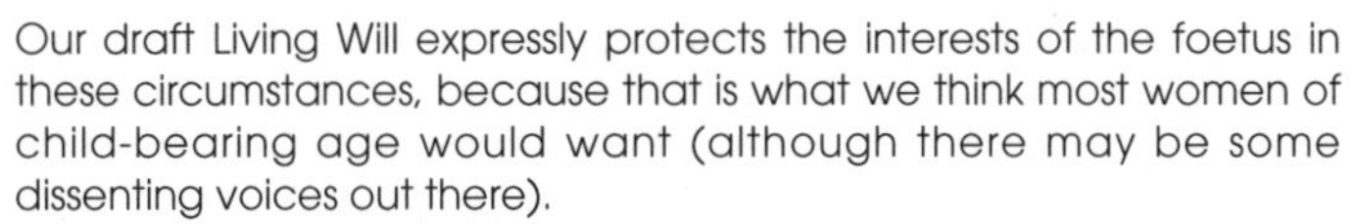

Our draft Living Will expressly protects the interests of the foetus in these circumstances, because that is what we think most women of child-bearing age would want (although there may be some dissenting voices out there).

For the dissenters, the Euthanasia Society of Scotland (see 'Useful contacts') publishes a living will on their website which asks doctors to carry out the advance directive regardless of the interests of the foetus.

Suppose I make a living will but when I fall ill some time later, a cure for my condition is just around the corner?

Up until the time when you lose **mental capacity**, you can always choose to revoke or amend your living will, and it is sensible to review it regularly in the light of your changing feelings and the advancement of medical science.

In theory, you might lose out if your living will prevented you from being given treatment which might have helped you. However, our draft Living Will provides that, if a cure is imminent, treatment will be continued.

Can I revoke my living will?

Yes, as long as, of course, you have the **mental capacity** to do so. You would need to write to your doctor and also let your immediate family know. Decisions about your treatment would then, if you became unable to decide for yourself, become your doctor 's responsibility in consultation with your family.

Can I amend my living will?

Yes, but do not try to alter an existing Living Will document, as this could create ambiguity and confusion at a time when clarity is all-important. The easy, foolproof way to change a living will is to print off a fresh one from the website, get it signed and witnessed (see Chapter 5) and *send copies to your doctor with a request to destroy the old one.*

Should I update my living will?

Yes. The longer the time between the making and the implementation of a living will, the greater will be the concern that it is out of date and does not reflect your current intentions. This is particularly the case where a living will is made by a young person in rude health who might be less tolerant of the prospect of disability and illness than an older person.

We suggest that you review your living will periodically, and particularly if you fall ill, to make sure it still reflects your intentions. We provide for this in our draft Living Will.

I understand that repeated doses of strong pain-killing drugs can shorten life. Does this amount to *physician assisted suicide?*

It may do so if the medication is not in your best interests. The question that then arises is what, in the circumstances, are really your best interests – to be kept alive despite the pain, or to be given pain relief which may hasten your death? The problem is even more acute if at the time you do not have **mental capacity** to decide for yourself. We address this issue in our draft Living Will, which asks for you to be given appropriate pain relief or other symptom relief, even though that relief may shorten your life. Furthermore, our Living Will says 'I release those looking after me from all liability arising from carrying out my instructions in this Living Will'.

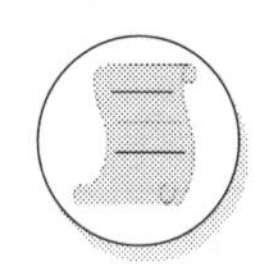

In 1999, Dr David Moor, a Northumberland GP, gave a massive dose of diamorphine to a terminally ill 85-year-old man. The diamorphine relieved his pain but it also killed him. Dr Moor openly admitted doing this and was prosecuted for murder. In May 1999 he was tried and acquitted. This verdict established that doctors who give drugs to relieve pain are acting lawfully, even if the drugs shorten the patient's life (the 'doctrine of double effect').

Is a living will an instruction to the medical team to abandon me to my fate regardless of the pain and indignity I may suffer?

No. **Basic care** must continue until you die, even though **medical treatment** may cease. Our Living Will asks for basic care to continue as long as life lasts.

Are there circumstances in which doctors can disregard a valid living will?

Yes:

- if you refuse **basic care**;
- if they believe that complying with your wishes will harm someone else – the obvious example being your unborn child;
- if you are suffering from an infectious disease which might put other people at risk if medical treatment were to be withdrawn.

Can a living will authorise the doctors to withdraw artificial feeding if I am in a persistent vegetative state?

No, not on its own. The view of the court is that starving someone to death is a crime, unless *the court says it isn't*! Thus feeding can be withdrawn only if the court so orders. The court will, however, take account of a **living will** which addresses the issue (our draft does).

Will the doctors take my living will into account in an emergency?

Yes – *if they know there is a living will in existence*. The problem, of course, is that in an emergency there may not be time to start hunting for it. In practice, therefore, the doctors will treat you first and hunt later.

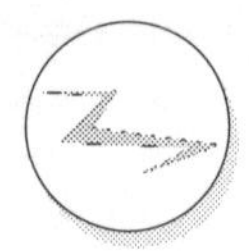

See page 41 for a 'living will card' that you can carry about with you so that doctors can find out your views without wasting precious time.

Can I write an *advance consent* that demands certain kinds of medical treatment?

You can try, and your wishes will be taken into account, but they will not be binding in the same way as an **advance refusal** would. The Welsh Office puts it very well: 'You may want to write down the sorts of treatment that you would rather have, and the concerns that you have about other kinds. These wishes would not be binding in the same way as an advance refusal. You cannot, for example, insist on a particular kind of treatment if a health care professional does not believe it is right for you. But if the time ever comes when you can no longer make decisions or tell people about them, it would help people providing health care to have your wishes as a guide when deciding what is in your best interests.'

How long does a living will remain valid after signing?

Your **living will** doesn't have a sell-by date. It will remain in force unless you cancel it while you have the **mental capacity** to do so.

Why might you need a living will?

WE Henley described Death as 'the ruffian on the stair'. But is Death always such a ruffian? Might we not sometimes, if we are allowed, welcome him as a kind and compassionate friend?

In the days before antibiotics, pneumonia usually meant a death sentence for a frail, bedridden old person. The discovery of antibiotics changed all that – and brought with it some uncomfortable choices. Here is a real life example.

> ... My father had suffered a severe stroke. He was paralysed, incontinent, unable to communicate. Then he developed pneumonia. The doctors could cure his pneumonia with antibiotics, but Dad would remain helpless and bedridden for the rest of his life.
> Dad would hate that, and I told the doctor so. This was in the days before anyone talked about living wills, but Dad had once written me a letter setting out his views about life and death. It was a thoughtful, loving letter and I carried it about with family photographs in my wallet. I showed Dad's letter to the doctor ... Dad was beautifully cared for, but he was not given antibiotics. He died peacefully and with dignity, just as he had hoped to.

This was someone who had made his wishes known beforehand and, when the time came, had them granted. That is what living wills are about. It's *your* decision.

Treatment with 'informed' consent

In general, sick people are entitled to refuse treatment for themselves. Treatment requires *consent* where the patient is able to give it. The **BMA** (British Medical Association) says:

> In most cases, health professionals cannot legally examine or treat any adult without his or her valid consent ... It is unlawful and unethical to treat a person who is capable of understanding and willing to know, without first explaining the nature of the procedure, its purpose and implications and obtaining that person's agreement.

An adult who has **mental capacity** has a legal right

- to receive information about their condition and options for medical treatment, and
- to decide for themselves whether to consent to treatment or, as long as no one else is put at risk, to refuse it.

Conversely, a doctor who persists with **medical treatment** against your known wishes may be guilty of assault.

Treatment with 'uninformed' consent

There are, of course, people who say 'Just go ahead. I'd rather not know the details'. The BMA accepts this: 'Their uninformed consent is valid *as long as they had the option of receiving more information*.' So you do not, therefore, have an obligation to make, or participate in, decisions about your medical treatment. You can leave it to the medical team to do what they consider to be necessary and in your best interests.

Treatment without consent

Not all treatment requires the patient's consent. This is particularly important in a medical emergency such as a road traffic accident where, for example, an otherwise competent patient may be temporarily unconscious.

If a patient is not 'capable of understanding', the doctors have to decide whether the procedure is

- 'necessary' *and*
- 'in the patient's best interests',

and if is the answer to both is 'yes', they will normally carry out the treatment as if the patient had agreed to it. Not only do doctors have the *right* to give treatment in these circumstances, they have a common law *duty* to do so.

Treatment despite refusal of consent

There are circumstances in which you will be treated even if you refuse, because following your instructions would harm someone else or put them at risk. The main instances are where you are suffering from an infectious disease, or are pregnant with a viable foetus.

The law also holds that children under the age of 18 and some mental patients are incapable of making a valid decision about their treatment. In these cases, the patient's 'best interests' will be paramount. This is not to say that the patient's views will be ignored. On the contrary, doctors will, in assessing the patient's best interests, take their wishes into account (but may not give them what they want if it is not appropriate for them).

In *Re W (A Minor)*, a 16-year-old girl with anorexia was judged to be mentally competent, but still had her refusal of treatment overruled.

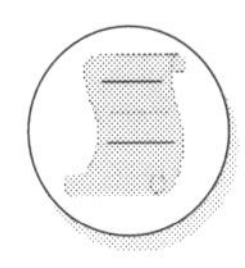

The right to decide *in advance*

It is all very well having a right to decide whether to accept or refuse medical treatment, but what if you do not have the **mental capacity** to decide at the time when you are ill?

You make a living will when you *do* have mental capacity.

What is a living will?

We have seen already that a living will is an advance refusal of **medical treatment** (but not **basic care** – see above) that you intend to have effect if and when:

- you lack the physical capacity to communicate your refusal; *or*
- you lack the **mental capacity** to refuse treatment; *and in either case*
- your quality of life is very poor; *and*
- there is no hope of recovery or even significant improvement.

A living will can, however, take various forms, including:

- a statement made by someone in good health – typically written a long time in advance – to cover all conceivable future eventualities;
- a statement made by a sick person, whose illness may be terminal. A statement in these circumstances may be better informed, more realistic, more relevant and more specific than one made from a perspective of rude health;
- a statement of personal life-and-death values – but this may place a considerable burden of interpretation on your family and on a busy medical team.

There is no **statutory** framework or standard form for living wills but, all the same, the law accepts that your living will is binding on your doctors as long as your requests meet the following seven conditions. The mnemonic here is **MEDICAL**.

M ental capacity

E thics – you must not ask doctors to do anything which is not allowed by their code of practice (for example, you cannot refuse **basic care**)

D uress-free – a living will made under undue influence or compulsion is not valid

I nformed – the result of relevant information and careful thought

C lear – so there is no doubt about your intentions

A pplicable to your medical condition at the time the living will comes into force

L awful – you must not ask for anything which is against the law (such as, for example, **physician assisted suicide**)

To meet these conditions, a living will requires careful consideration. It is not something to dash off casually or, even worse, in a blind panic.

A living will is *not*:

- a request for **basic care** to be withdrawn;
- a request for **voluntary euthanasia** or **physician assisted suicide**.

The Prime Minister, Tony Blair, made this clear in 1997:

> Contrary to what some have tried to assert, an **advance directive** is not a move towards legalising euthanasia. It is a way for patients to reinforce their right to refuse treatment by anticipating a time when they may lose the capacity to make or convey the decision. *An advance directive cannot authorise a medical practitioner to do anything which is illegal* [emphasis added].

The last sentence is the most important. People become doctors because they want to heal patients, not kill them. Physician assisted suicide is a crime, and procuring this for yourself or anyone else is also a criminal offence in the UK.

The BMA says that it:

> ... respects the autonomy of competent patients to refuse life-prolonging/sustaining medical treatment and intervention (either contemporaneously or by advance directive).

It does, however, draw a clear distinction between respecting patients' rights to refuse treatment and actively ending their lives:

> Doctors should accede to a request not to prolong the patient's life by provision of treatment which the patient does not want, but *the BMA's policy … is that doctors should not actively intervene to end life or give assistance to this end* [emphasis added].

So there you have it: the BMA accept that

- a competent adult can refuse treatment, *but*
- medical ethics do not allow a doctor to hasten their death.

Why isn't euthanasia legal?

Living wills are, in many people's minds, closely associated with **euthanasia**. If you type 'living will' into a search engine on the internet, you will find several sites devoted to euthanasia, **physician assisted suicide** and the like (see 'Useful contacts'). Some of these sites are sincere, informative and thought-provoking and make a strong and moving case for legalising euthanasia. Euthanasia, after all, means 'good death', the peaceful, painless end for which we all hope. Why, then, has it not been made legal in the UK?

A House of Lords Select Committee on Medical Ethics was established in the wake of the 'Bland case' (see p 7). In their report, they recognised that we all 'hope for an easy death without suffering, dementia or dependence', and they listened to many arguments in favour of fulfilling that hope through euthanasia. They then made two important points.

(1) The prohibition against intentional killing is fundamental to the rule of law

The House of Lords recognised that there could be instances where there is a conflict of interests between society, for which any relaxation in the prohibition may be harmful, and the individual, who may crave release from a burdensome and painful existence. It went on to say that the interests of society should prevail:

> Ultimately we do not believe that the arguments are sufficient reason to weaken society's prohibition of intentional killing. That prohibition is the cornerstone of law and of social relationships. It protects each one of us impartially, embodying the belief that all are equal ... Dying is not only a personal or individual affair. The death of a person affects the lives of others.

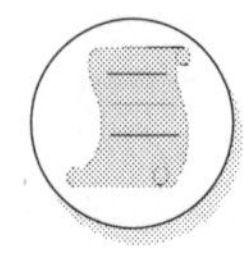

The law on euthanasia was put to the test in 2001–02 by Mrs Diane Pretty. Mrs Pretty was terminally ill with motor neurone disease. She was fearful that in the final stages of her illness she would suffer a painful and terrifying death by slow suffocation. She wanted to die before the illness reached that stage, but she was already paralysed from the neck down and could not commit suicide unaided. She wanted her husband, Brian, to be allowed (as she put it) to 'help her die', and in August 2001 she asked the Director of Public Prosecutions to grant Mr Pretty immunity from prosecution if he ended her life. The DPP refused.

Supported by pro-euthanasia groups, Mrs Pretty went to court, arguing that the DPP's decision was an infringement of her human rights. She fought her case unsuccessfully first in the High Court, then in the House of Lords, while the pro-euthanasia and pro-life groups watched anxiously. Finally, in the spring of 2002, Mrs Pretty took her case to the European Court of Human Rights. To the pro-life groups' relief and the pro-euthanasia lobby's disappointment, the European judges dismissed her claim.

In May 2002, Mrs Pretty was admitted to a hospice near her home, where she died. Euthanasia and assisted suicide are still unlawful in the UK.

---

(2) Vulnerable people must be protected

If euthanasia were allowed, the old, the lonely and the sick would feel pressured to ask for it. One thing leads to another: how do you set a limit? The House of Lords felt that we were at the top of a very slippery slope. A shrewd push could send us hurtling down.

> We do not think it possible to set secure limits on voluntary euthanasia. Some witnesses told us that to legalise voluntary euthanasia was a discrete [separate] step which need have no other consequences. But issues of life and death do not lend themselves to clear definition ... It would be next to impossible to ensure that all acts of

euthanasia were truly voluntary and that any liberalisation of the law was not abused.

If **voluntary euthanasia**, **physician-assisted suicide** or whatever you care to call it became legal, this would change people's attitudes to anyone with long-term illness, dementia or disability. There is already a great deal of talk about 'bed-blockers' and 'benefit scroungers'. It is all too easy to imagine a society in which long-term sick and disabled people were encouraged to end their lives, supposedly for the common good. Many science fiction and future history stories describe societies where euthanasia is compulsory for the old, the physically handicapped and the mentally infirm. There have, of course, been régimes that advocated precisely this. The Nazi catch-phrase was 'life unworthy of life'. Anyone who seriously advocates euthanasia has to address how we are to avoid the wickedness of the Nazi past.

The **BMA**, on behalf of doctors, has its own objections to voluntary euthanasia. It makes the point that 'if doctors were authorised to carry out euthanasia or physician assisted suicide, however carefully circumscribed the situation, they would acquire an additional role to the traditional one of healer'. As a distinguished American lawyer, Alexander Capron, puts it:

> I never want to have to wonder whether the physician coming into my hospital room is wearing the white coat of the healer ... or the black hood of the executioner. Trust between patient and physician is simply too important and too fragile to be subjected to the unnecessary strain.

What is more, **voluntary euthanasia** is, in fact, a form of suicide. Anyone who has experienced the aftermath of someone's suicide will know how much misery and turmoil suicide causes for those who are left behind. Many people who commit suicide are mentally ill or suffering overwhelming emotional distress. All the same, suicide is a selfish act; to plan one's suicide while mentally competent is, arguably, the ultimate betrayal of family and friends.

The moral arguments which apply against suicide apply equally to voluntary euthanasia. As we have said, *a living will is not a licence to kill.*

It is pointless to ask for anything in your living will which would conflict with health professionals' ethics, because they would not be able to grant it. The BMA says, 'One of the important points about this type of statement is that it shows that advance decision-making concerns a right to choose rather than a right to die'.

What next?

The moral landscape is different in Switzerland and the Netherlands, where euthanasia is legal under strictly controlled conditions. There, the individual's right to choose the time and manner of their death is seen as paramount, and not to be denied for the greater good of society, religious doctrine or the ethical scruples of medical professionals.

The organisation *Dignitas* arranges trips to Switzerland with suicide as the main attraction, and several British people have taken advantage of this. Moreover, at the time of writing a Private Member's Bill to legalise euthanasia in the United Kingdom has been introduced in the House of Lords by Lord Joffé. So far, the standard of debate we have seen on this subject is not impressive – most people seem to see it as a chance to take their hobby horses for a brisk canter rather than an opportunity to thoroughly explore the issues.

Arguments for and against making a living will

> Let an advance directive [a living will] speak for you. It's your voice and your gift to your family. By addressing end-of-life issues, you lift a tremendous burden from them.
>
> *Marge Reed of the Mayo Clinic*

The ability to make decisions for and about ourselves is the key to our sense of dignity and self esteem. Accident or serious illness can strike without warning. A living will is in your own interests because it empowers you in a situation where you would otherwise be powerless, and it protects you from indignity and suffering.

In addition, a living will can help other people. It can:

- give guidance to professionals and reduce doubt and uncertainty in a distressing and bewildering situation;
- prevent family disagreements about what you would and would not have wanted;
- give comfort and reassurance to the people who love you.

Living wills are much more common in America than in Britain – for the unmeritorious reason that health care in the USA is costly and people do not want to linger on at enormous expense!

Arguments against making a living will

Many people think that living wills travel with sinister baggage. Pro-life groups object to living wills in principle as being contrary to the sanctity of life. Muslim pro-life supporters, for example, believe that only Allah should choose the time when we die. Those Roman Catholics who object to living wills see them as sinful for the same reason that they object to suicide: in the words of the sixth Commandment, *Thou shalt not kill.*

There are also reasons of practical morality for treating living wills with caution. If living wills become the norm, vulnerable people may feel under pressure 'not to be a burden'. This pressure may come from the family – who want to be spared the expense and inconvenience, or it may come from social expectation – you don't want to be seen as a scrounger, a bed-blocker or a general party-pooper by lingering on for longer than seems proper. It is all very well to say that living wills made under duress are ineffective, but who is to know what subtle influences are brought to bear on frail and vulnerable people?

Then there are reasons of self-interest – and why not? Many people may not fully understand what they are asking for in refusing medical treatment. For example:

- We know from the 'Bland case' (see p 7) that nutrition can be a form of **medical treatment** as opposed to **basic care**. Do you really want to be starved to death?
- What about withdrawal of **hydration**? According to a letter to *The Times* by Gerard Wright, QC, 'There are strong grounds for believing that an unconscious and vegetative person who is deprived of hydration will suffer all the pangs of thirst and die in agony'.
- Your views about your condition and treatment may well change over a period of time, and what you once saw as unthinkable may gradually become more acceptable.

The House of Lords Select Committee on medical ethics said:

> Disabled individuals are commonly more satisfied with their life than able-bodied people would expect to be with the same disability. The healthy do not choose in the same way as the sick.

In an article in *The Times*, Doctor Thomas Stuttaford summed up this view when he wrote:

> Whereas to a young doctor the quality of life of these patients may seem so low as to be not worth keeping, most of the patients are very grateful for what life they have.

Can you be sure you will not change your mind too? A particularly alarming scenario may occur if you change your mind but cannot communicate it, or if you fail to amend or revoke a previous living will. A young person writing a living will now may even forget they ever did so, and find themselves being denied treatment 30 or 40 years later.

- Medical science does not stand still. You may, in your living will, refuse treatment for an illness which at the time was a death sentence, but which is routinely curable a few years later.
- There are documented accounts of people recovering after months and even years in a coma. Who is to say that by making a living will refusing treatment for such a condition, you will not be losing out on a chance to recover, however unlikely this might seem at the time?

You should not make a living will unless you are aware of all these considerations and are still satisfied that *a living will is right for you.*

Legal considerations

Living wills, as opposed to **euthanasia** or **physician assisted suicide**, are legal. The courts have in recent years determined that a living will made *in advance,* which expresses your wishes clearly and is applicable to your case, will be as effective as a request made *at the time.*

Why, then, does a living will *not* have **statutory** force in the UK? In other words, why is there no 'Living Wills Act'?

The Government line (spin, even) is that no statute is necessary because existing law, conveniently supported by the BMA Code of Practice, is adequate. According to the Government, its reason for not passing a law about living wills has nothing to do with the fact that it may be controversial. This is all very well, but the issues involved in living wills seem to have galloped ahead of the law and there is a good argument that some official guidance would help and protect both patients and doctors. Under current law, for example, doctors are at risk of prosecution for assault if they treat a patient against their will, but face criminal charges if they help the patient to die. Is this fair to anyone?

In general, people *do* have the right to refuse **medical treatment**, but not in every case (see Chapter 1). There are certain **statutory** exceptions. For example, if you are suffering from a severe mental illness which makes you a danger to others, the authorities have **statutory** powers under the Mental Health Acts (there are several) to treat you and detain you in hospital against your wishes. In such cases, the Mental Health Acts would override your living will.

A valid living will

We have set out in Chapter 2 the seven conditions which must be satisfied for a living will to be valid. The mnemonic, you will recall, is **MEDICAL**:

- **M** ental capacity
- **E** thics – you must not ask doctors to do anything which is not allowed by their code of practice (for example, you cannot refuse **basic care**)
- **D** uress-free – a living will made under undue influence or compulsion is not valid
- **I** nformed – the result of relevant information and careful thought
- **C** lear – so there is no doubt about your intentions
- **A** pplicable to your medical condition at the time the living will comes into force
- **L** awful – you must not ask for anything which is against the law (such as, for example, **physician assisted suicide**)

Our draft Living Will is *lawful, ethical* and (we hope) *clear.* It will come into effect if and when it is *applicable* to your medical condition at the time. However, the other conditions depend on you.

Mental capacity – the right to be wrong

Mental capacity can be an elusive, subtle creature, hard to pin down. Doctors and other professionals, such as lawyers, have to assess clients' mental capacity every day and usually they have little difficulty in deciding whether someone has the mental capacity for a given purpose or is 'several jewels short of a tiara'. However, there are special considerations in the context of living wills. For example, your mental sharpness may be blurred by physical illness or medication.

If you have read thus far, we would judge that you have the mental capacity to make a living will – but it would be tragic if, once you were sick and helpless, someone challenged your competence to do so on the grounds that *they* thought you were making the wrong choice. Fortunately, the law acknowledges that people can have the mental capacity to understand something and then go on to make a thoroughly dodgy decision about it. The BMA says:

> It is irrelevant whether the refusal [of treatment] is contrary to the views of most other people or whether the person lacks insight into other aspects of life as long as he or she is able to decide on the one matter in question.

When a psychotic patient in Broadmoor refused to allow his gangrenous foot to be amputated, the High Court upheld his refusal, although the man's views on other matters were not – shall we say – in accordance with reality.

Dame Elizabeth Butler-Sloss 'blessed' this freedom to get things wrong when she said:

> A man or woman of full age and sound understanding may choose to reject medical advice and medical or surgical treatment either partially or in its entirety. A decision to refuse medical treatment by a patient capable of making the decision does not have to be sensible, rational or well considered ...

Of course, it is easy to say that everyone has the right to be irrational, but an irrational decision tends to suggest that the decider lacked **mental capacity** (Catch 22)! If you want to make a decision which others are likely to find bizarre, consider obtaining a medical opinion about your **mental capacity** and enclose the report with your Living Will.

In general, to demonstrate mental capacity for the purpose of making a living will you should be able to

- gather information (see above),
- analyse that information, and
- make a decision (even if nobody else agrees with it).

If Dame Elizabeth Butler-Sloss says it's OK to make a wrong decision, that should be good enough for anyone!

Duress-free – is this your own choice, made free of duress or undue influence?

A living will which is not made freely is not valid.

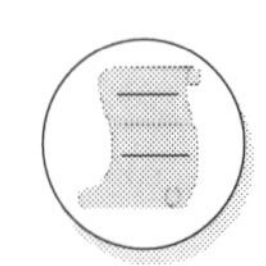

In *Re T (Adult: Refusal of Treatment)*, a Jehovah's Witness, who was critically injured in a road accident and who had refused a blood transfusion, was given one without her consent after her father and boyfriend obtained a court ruling that the transfusion would not be unlawful. The court held that although the patient was not mentally ill, her physical condition, together with misinformation and the influence of her mother, had made her refusal of treatment ineffective.

Informed – do you have all the information you need to make a reasoned decision?

Take time to find out as much as you can, particularly about any illness that you are already suffering from. You should aim to know:

- what medical treatment is being offered, why it is being offered and what it is intended to do;
- the main benefits and risks;
- the various options;
- what is likely to happen if you do not receive the proposed treatment.

Help and advice are available. Health professionals are strongly encouraged to take time to talk to their patients and discuss all the treatment options. Some hospitals employ special counsellors and there may also be outreach services and community nurses to help you towards an 'informed decision'.

One of the reasons we recommend that you review your living will periodically is so that you can show that your decisions are based on current information about your medical condition and that your instructions still apply.

How to make a living will

Let us suppose that you have now decided that a living will is right for you.

If you want to use our draft Living Will (see Chapter 6), do read it through carefully first to check that it says what you want it to say and is applicable to your circumstances. Remember that there is no prescribed form of living will. If you are already suffering from what you know is a terminal illness, you may well want to write something which is highly specific about what treatments you will and will not accept. If in any doubt at all, seek professional advice.

Take the time to read this Living Will carefully, and fill in all the boxes. Tick only when you are sure. The purpose of the boxes is to make sure that you give informed consideration to every item. Only then will your living will meet the seven conditions to make it valid:

M ental capacity
E thics
D uress-free
I nformed
C lear
A pplicable
L awful

Signing your living will

How it's done

First, find two impartial witnesses. The following must *not* witness your Living Will:

- your husband, wife or partner;
- a relative;
- anyone who stands to gain by your death (for example, by inheriting something in your will).

Two neighbours would be ideal. The procedure is as follows:

(1) You sign the Living Will first, in ink, with both witnesses watching. *There is no need for them to read it or even to know what the document is about.*

(2) Both witnesses then sign the Living Will, with you watching.

(3) You date your Living Will with the date of signing.

(4) Both you and the witnesses should now initial the bottom right-hand corner of each page, except the page on which you sign.

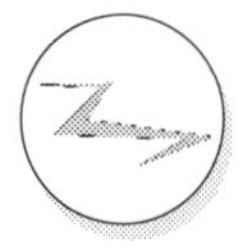

Remember – the witnesses are signing to say that *they have seen you sign your name*. They do *not* need to know what the document is about.

Two 'don'ts'

- *Don't* cross anything out or make any alterations either before or after signing. They could make your Living Will invalid. If you make a mistake, start again.
- Don't try to add a 'PS' after signing. It could be very confusing for everyone. If you want to make any changes or additions, start again.

Letting people know

There is no point in keeping your Living Will to yourself. At the very least you must give a copy to

- your family doctor, *and*
- any specialist doctor in charge of your case (for example, if you are in hospital), *and*
- a trusted friend or member of your family.

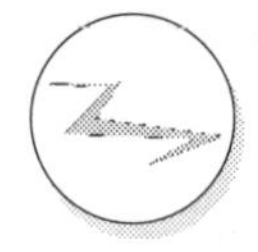

Carry a card

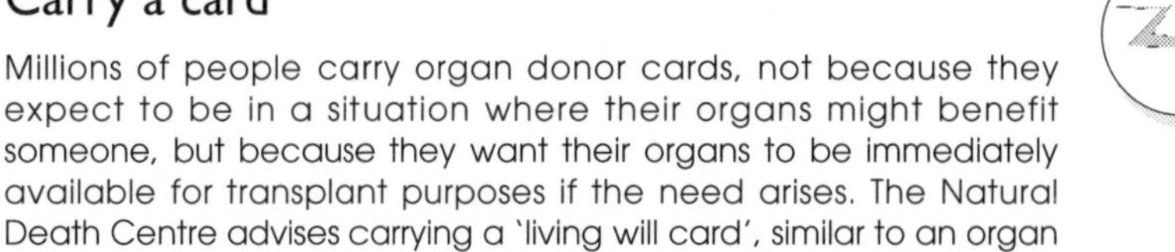

Millions of people carry organ donor cards, not because they expect to be in a situation where their organs might benefit someone, but because they want their organs to be immediately available for transplant purposes if the need arises. The Natural Death Centre advises carrying a 'living will card', similar to an organ donor card, to let people know that you have made a living will. Suggested wording is:

> LIVING WILL: I have made a Living Will stating that, if I fall terminally ill, I do not wish to have my life prolonged by medical interventions. My Living Will is lodged with Doctor (name) of (address and tel no) and with (name) of (address and tel no).

There is a sample card on the website for you to download.

Storing your living will

There is no point in keeping your Living Will in a place which, although safe, is not obvious or accessible. Many living wills are never required, but if yours is needed, it *is* absolutely vital to make sure your doctor and your immediate family know that you have made a Living Will and where to find it in a hurry.

A living will/advance request *must* be kept separate from your will itself, otherwise nobody will know about it until it's too late.

A draft living will

You can find this on the website (see p ii), and can download as many copies as you need.

ABOUT ME

My name: ....

My address: ....

MY MENTAL CAPACITY

I believe that I have the mental capacity to make this Living Will. This is to say, I possess the mental ability to gather relevant information (for example, about any medical condition from which I may suffer), analyse that information, and make the decisions which are set out here.

Although I may be unwell at the time of making my Living Will, my mental capacity for this task is not clouded by illness, pain, anxiety or medication.

Yes, I have mental capacity ❑

MY FREEDOM OF CHOICE

I am making this Living Will voluntarily, free from undue influence, pressure or duress. This is my decision and mine alone.

Yes, this is my own decision ❑

MY MEDICAL CONDITION

(Option 1)

If I am in good health at the time making this Living Will, I understand that if I fall ill I may have a different view of what is and is not an acceptable quality of life, but all the same I intend this Living Will to be binding.

Yes, I intend my Living Will to be binding ❑

or

(Option 2)

If I am already in poor health at the time of making this Living Will, I understand the implications of my medical condition, the likely outcome and the treatment options available to me.

Yes, I understand the implications ❑

DEFINITIONS

When I use the following terms in my Living Will, this is what I intend them to mean:

'**basic care**' – care essential to keep me comfortable.

This includes warmth, shelter, pain relief, management of distressing symptoms such as breathlessness and vomiting, hygienic measures, such as management of incontinence, and the offer of oral nutrition and hydration.

Yes, this is what I mean by 'basic care' ❑

'**medical treatmen**t' – medical intervention to alleviate my medical condition or prevent its deterioration.

I understand this to include everything from examination and diagnostic tests through surgery and courses of drugs to physiotherapy and rehabilitation, and may also include artificial nutrition and hydration.

Yes, this is what I mean by 'medical treatment' ❑

'**artificial nutrition and hydration**' – the giving of food and water other than by mouth.

Yes, this is what I mean by 'artificial nutrition and hydration' ❑

WHEN MY LIVING WILL IS TO BECOME EFFECTIVE

I intend my Living Will to become effective when:

- I am suffering from one or more of the medical conditions listed in this Living Will *and*
- I have no realistic prospect of recovery or even of significant improvement *and*
- I have permanently lost the mental capacity to make decisions concerning my treatment, *and/or*
- I have permanently lost the physical capacity to communicate my wishes concerning my treatment.

Yes, this is when I intend my Living Will to become effective ❑

MEDICAL CONDITIONS

The medical conditions I have in mind are:

- cancer
  Yes ❑ *No* ❑
- AIDS or other immune deficiency
  Yes ❑ *No* ❑
- multiple sclerosis, motor neurone disease, Parkinson's disease or any other disease of the nervous system
  Yes ❑ *No* ❑
- mental impairment caused by injury, stroke, senile or pre-senile dementia, disease, or any other cause
  Yes ❑ *No* ❑
- persistent vegetative state or similar condition
  Yes ❑ *No* ❑
- any other equally serious or disabling medical condition
  Yes ❑ *No* ❑
- any medical condition from which I am suffering at the time of making this Living Will, and which I specify in the box below *(note: if you can't think of anything, leave the box empty)*

MY ADVANCE REFUSAL OF MEDICAL TREATMENT

In any of the circumstances specified above, and subject to my further instructions below, I refuse medical treatment *unless a cure for my condition is imminent.*

Yes, I refuse ❑

MY FURTHER INSTRUCTIONS

I wish to receive basic care until my life ends, and I instruct those responsible for me as follows:

- If I am suffering from pain or distress, I am to receive appropriate pain relief or other treatment, even though that pain relief or treatment may shorten my life.
  Yes ❑ *No* ❑
- If withdrawing artificial nutrition and/or hydration would cause me pain or distress, I wish them to continue.
  Yes ❑ *No* ❑

- If I should be in a persistent vegetative state or similar condition, but measures to end my life cannot be taken without a court order, the contents of this Living Will are to be made known to those responsible for the decision.
  Yes ❑ *No* ❑

- If, while suffering from any of the conditions listed above, I contract a further, curable illness, I refuse medical treatment for this illness. *(For example, you could add: if I have senile dementia and then contract pneumonia, I am not to receive treatment for the pneumonia.)*
  Yes, I refuse ❑ *No* ❑

PREGNANCY

If I am pregnant with a viable foetus at the time this Living Will comes into effect, the interests of the foetus are to prevail over mine. This means that medical treatment for me should continue until it can be withdrawn without threatening the life or health of my unborn child.

Yes, continue treatment ❑

No ❑

Not applicable ❑

ETHICS AND RESPONSIBILITY

I do not ask those looking after me to do anything which is unlawful or unethical with reference to the British Medical Association's Code of Conduct.

If my treatment is in the hands of someone who, for religious or ethical reasons, feels unable to comply with my instructions in this Living Will, I wish them to hand over my care to someone who is able to comply.

I release those looking after me from any liability that might arise from complying with the advance refusal of medical treatment in my Living Will.

Yes ❑ *No* ❑

INTERPRETATION

If in the future those looking after me are in doubt about how to apply the instructions in my Living Will to the circumstances which arise, they are to consult the person or persons named below, whose interpretation of my instructions is to be taken into consideration.

(This clause is optional. You don't have to name anyone if you don't want to.)

1 Name ....
Address ....
Telephone no ....
E-mail ....

2 Name ....
Address ....
Telephone no ....
E-mail ....

CANCELLATION

I have the right to cancel or change this Living Will while I have the mental capacity to do so. I will normally do this by marking this Living Will as cancelled, or destroying it. If I have sent copies of this Living Will to my doctor and/or family, I will inform them in writing about the cancellation.

Otherwise, they are to assume that my Living Will remains in force.

Yes ❑ *No* ❑

ADVICE

I have taken *(or have had the opportunity to take)* professional advice about my medical condition (if applicable) and the implications of this Living Will before signing it.

Yes ❑ *No* ❑

(Note: to tick the box here, you do not need to have taken advice, it is enough that you have had the chance to do so if you wanted. If your doctor gives you medical advice before you sign your Living Will, consider asking them to sign a certificate saying so. A specimen is provided on p 52)

SIGNING, WITNESSING AND DATING

I sign this Living Will to give it legal force, in the presence of two independent adult witnesses, neither of whom will profit by my death.

Signed on the .... day of .... 20 ....

....

My signature

Witness 1

Signature: ....

Full name: ....

Address: ....

Occupation: ....

Witness 2

Signature: ....

Full name: ....

Address: ....

Occupation: ....

REVIEW:

I confirm that I reviewed my Living Will on the date or dates below and I confirm that my instructions remain the same.

Date{s} of review: ....

....

My signature at date of review(s)

Alternative validations for someone unable to read and/or write

Suppose you cannot read your Living Will, because of blindness, illiteracy, etc, or because of disability you cannot write your signature?

Have no fear! As long as you have the **mental capacity** to do so, you can draw up a Living Will regardless of your ability to read or write, but you should use one of the signature clauses below.

- If you cannot read the document, it should be read to you and you should confirm that you understand it before it is signed.
- If you are unable to write, the document can be signed by someone else on your behalf.

Signature clause for someone who is blind or otherwise unable to read, but can still sign

As I am unable to read, my Living Will has been read aloud to me. I understand and approve it. By signing this Living Will I intend to give it legal force and I sign it in the presence of two independent adult witnesses, neither of whom will profit by my death.

Signed on the .... day of .... 20 ....

....

My signature

Witness 1

Signature: ....

Full name: ....

Address: ....

Occupation: ....

Witness 2

Signature: ....

Full name: ....

Address: ....

Occupation: ....

Signature clause for someone unable to write

As I am unable to write, I have authorised .... to give my Living Will legal force by signing it in my presence and in the presence of the two witnesses named below, neither of whom will profit by my death, and both of them have signed it in my presence.

Signed on the .... day of .... 20 ....

....

My signature

Witness 1

Signature: ....

Full name: ....

Address: ....

Occupation: ....

Witness 2

Signature: ....

Full name: ....

Address: ....

Occupation: ....

Signature clause for someone who is unable to read *and* unable to write

As I am unable to read, my Living Will has been read aloud to me. I understand and approve it.

As I am unable to write, I have authorised .... to give my Living Will legal force by signing it in my presence and in the presence of the two witnesses named below, neither of whom will profit from my death, and both of them have signed it in my presence.

Signed on the .... day of .... 20 ....

....

My signature

Witness 1

Signature: ....

Full name: ....

Address: ....

Occupation: ....

Witness 2

Signature: ....

Full name: ....

Address: ....

Occupation: ....

DOCTOR'S CERTIFICATE

Date of certificate: ....

Name of doctor: ....

Address of doctor: ....

Name of patient ('the patient'): ....

Patient's National Insurance no: ....

- I confirm that I have responsibility for the patient's medical treatment; *and*
- I confirm that the patient consulted me on (*date*) with a view to making a living will; *and*
- I am satisfied that, at the time of the consultation:
  - the patient understood the implications of their medical condition, the likely outcome and the treatment options; *and*
  - the patient had the mental capacity to make a living will.

....

Doctor's signature

And finally ...

Have you made sure that everyone who needs to know about your living will has a copy? These are likely to include:

- family members;
- your doctor;
- your carer (if applicable);
- the hospital looking after you (if applicable).

PART 2

ENDURING POWERS OF ATTORNEY

Buzzwords

Here are some terms you will come across in this Part. Please do not skip this section, as many of the terms used by lawyers have special meanings. Here we make them clear. The terms appear in **bold** in the text.

agent – a person to whom you give authority to act for you, which usually extends to negotiating and/or entering into contracts on your behalf. Pop stars use agents to get them the best recording contracts; ordinary folk use estate agents to negotiate property deals. In benefit-speak, an agent is someone who collects your state benefits for you (see p 79). An *attorney* is a kind of agent, but a special one (see below).

appointee – benefit-speak for someone, usually a close relative or friend, who can deal with your state benefits if you lack the mental capacity to do so for yourself.

attorney – in this context, we are not talking about American lawyers, the District Attorney (DA) or even the Attorney General.

'Attorney' simply means 'someone who is appointed'. It comes from the old French 'attourner' – to turn or hand over to someone else.

An attorney is someone to whom you give legal powers over your affairs by *deed* (see below). The powers may be limited – for example, to just signing documents while you are away, or comprehensive – to include the power to make important decisions about your affairs on your behalf.

An attorney under an enduring power of attorney (Continuing Power of Attorney in Scotland) has powers which are both limited and extended by statute as well as those granted by you.

Court of Protection – an office of the Supreme Court whose function is to give orders to administer the property and finances of people who do not have the *mental capacity* to manage their own affairs.

deed – a legal document which is signed, witnessed and delivered as a deed. The distinguishing feature of a deed used to be that it had a seal (see below), but this requirement has been abolished so that nowadays its only distinguishing feature is that it calls itself a 'deed'! An *Enduring Power of Attorney* (EPA) is a deed. It even says on the document 'Signed as a deed and delivered'. Trust us. But who it is supposed to be delivered to is a mystery.

We often say that a document has been 'signed, sealed and delivered'. This goes back to the days when important documents required a seal – an impression in molten wax of a heavy brass, silver or gold die – as well as a signature. Anyone who has seen old deeds in museums or archives will know how elaborate these seals could be. Even ordinary letters were sealed with sealing-wax and the molten wax stamped with the sender's own seal, often kept on a watch chain or worn on a ring. If the seal had been broken, your letter had been tampered with.

Today you can still buy seals at any law stationer, but the cheap ones are merely self-adhesive discs and, however much legal clout they may have, they lack gravitas. You do not, however, need a seal for an Enduring Power of Attorney – they did away with this requirement when the Law of Property (Miscellaneous Provisions) Act came into effect in 1990.

---

donor – (in this context) someone who confers (gives) a power of attorney. Other words for donor are *grantor* and *principal*. By analogy, the attorney is sometimes called a *donee* or *grantee*.

enduring powers of attorney (EPAs) – the legal authority which you give to someone so that they can handle your financial affairs even if you become mentally incapable of doing so. This is done by means of a prescribed form of document, or *deed* (see above), which is itself known as an Enduring Power of Attorney (EPA). By contrast to an *enduring* power of attorney, any other form of power of attorney becomes invalid if you lose *mental capacity*.

joint and several – joint as well as separate individual responsibility.

mental capacity – the ability to gather information, analyse it and make a decision. The level of mental capacity which is adequate for a particular task will depend upon its complexity. For example, you need a lower level of mental capacity to decide whether to have tea or coffee than to decide whether to hand over your financial affairs and, if so, to whom. These decisions in turn require less mental capacity than actually handling your financial affairs yourself.

Public Guardianship Office (PGO) – an executive agency within the Department for Constitutional Affairs, which deals with the management of the financial affairs of individuals who lack the mental capacity to do this themselves. The PGO does this on the authority of the Court of Protection (see 'Useful contacts').

receiver – the Court of Protection's name for someone appointed to administer the affairs of a mentally incompetent client who has not granted an enduring power of attorney.

short order – an order from the Court of Protection authorising someone (usually a family member) to act as receiver to handle the financial affairs of someone who has lost mental capacity and whose assets do not exceed £16,000.

statutory – laid down by law (statute) passed by Parliament, as opposed to 'judge-made' law (case law). The EPA form is a statutory document: creative writing is discouraged.

statutory will – a will made by the Court of Protection for a person without the mental capacity to make their own will (often referred to as 'testamentary capacity'). See p 94 for more details.

the 'two trustee rule' – the rule which prohibits a sole trustee from selling and otherwise dealing with trust assets. The concept is that two trustees will keep an eye on each other and there is less risk of abuse at the expense of beneficiaries and innocent people involved in the deal (see p 63).

Frequently asked questions (FAQs)

Note: the answers here apply only to enduring powers of attorney (EPAs). The position regarding other kinds of powers of attorney may be different.

I am 76 and I have been told I ought to give my children an enduring power of attorney. But I feel fine and have no wish to hand over the reins just yet. Will giving an EPA mean losing control?

No. You can give your children an EPA on the understanding that they will not exercise their power while you are still able to cope. You can, in fact, state specifically on your EPA form that the power will not come into force until the **attorneys** actually apply to the **Court of Protection** for the EPA to be registered (see Chapter 12).

I am mentally as alert as ever, but my sight is failing and I can't get about as I'd like. Would an EPA help?

An EPA is not just for people with failing **mental capacity** (although its great virtue is that it can continue even if your mental powers do fail).

Elderly people often appoint an **attorney** – typically a trusted son or daughter – to handle their financial affairs for them. They may be as mentally alert as ever, but if they have trouble getting about, or if their sight is not what it was, they may be glad to have someone to go to the bank for them or to write out cheques for them to sign, or, if the need arises, to buy and sell property on their behalf. An EPA is not strictly necessary for some of these tasks, but in practice it is useful to have a legal document to wave under the noses of the bureaucrats.

Do I actually need a formal legal document to ask my son to manage my financial affairs for me?

While you have **mental capacity**, your son can do a great deal of routine work for you on the basis of an oral request, although it is much better to have something in writing to forestall any arguments in the future about what was and was not agreed. A letter asking your son to act for you would normally be enough. He will then be your **agent**.

There are, however, some circumstances – even while you have mental capacity – in which you would need a formal **deed** giving your son a power of attorney, though not necessarily an enduring one, to perform certain transactions. These include transfers of land and leases for more than three years. Take professional advice in such cases.

If you lose mental capacity, no grant of powers short of an EPA will be sufficient to authorise your son to conduct your affairs.

I am an author and if I become mentally incompetent I would like my daughter to manage my ordinary financial affairs and my son to deal with literary matters such as permissions and royalties. Can I make more than one enduring power of attorney?

Yes. Some **donors** choose to make two or more EPAs appointing different attorneys to do different things.

You ought, however, to take professional advice to make sure that the different EPAs do what you wish them to do, and that your two attorneys work satisfactorily together.

My husband and I would like to make a joint enduring power of attorney. How can we do this?

You can't. There's no such thing. You will each have to make individual EPAs. The rule that only *individuals* can grant EPAs means that entities like companies and public authorities cannot grant EPAs either.

Can I change my mind once I have signed an EPA?

Yes. As long as you have **mental capacity**, you can cancel an EPA at any time. After you have become mentally incapable it is, of course, too late to cancel and the power will continue until you recover, or die, or until the **attorney** resigns, becomes incapable of acting for you, or dies.

I've changed my mind. How do I cancel my EPA?

There are two steps to cancellation. First, there must be an act of cancellation, preferably in writing. For example, you could write 'CANCELLED' in large letters across each page of the original (and also any copies you can get your hands on) and sign the cancellation. Secondly, you must notify your soon-to-be-ex attorney – again preferably in writing – that the power is cancelled. Keep a copy of your letter. If you still have mental capacity but can no longer physically write, you can get somebody else to do this for you.

If I sign an Enduring Power of Attorney, when can my attorney start acting for me?

Immediately. However, so long as you have mental capacity you can, if you choose, continue to manage your own affairs, letting your attorney(s) step in only when you need them.

Your attorney(s) will, of course, take over full time if and when you become mentally incapable. That is what your EPA is all about.

My son doesn't want to be my attorney unless I make it worth his while. Can I pay him for his trouble?

Yes. All attorneys are entitled to recover out-of-pocket expenses. If they are professionals, they will expect to charge a fee. As a matter of good practice, they should tell you their terms of business and charging rates in advance.

The problems with paying family members are:

- How much? You presumably do not wish to write a blank cheque, so if possible agree the rate in advance.
- What for? Do you intend to pay them to do things they would normally do for free?

If you do want your attorney to be paid you should say so on the form, so add above your signature:

'I intend that my attorney(s) should receive reasonable and proper remuneration for their services as attorney(s), including services of a personal nature.'

If you don't want to pay a family member but want them to have some financial reward, consider a legacy in your will (see *Wills and Estate Planning* in the *Pocket Lawyer* series).

(For more about paying attorneys, see 'Remuneration', p 95.)

Can my attorneys use my assets to benefit themselves?

In theory, no, other than

- by carrying on your wishes by benefiting other people (who may include the attorney) in the way you have in the past, or would in the future;
- by giving small presents to friends and relatives (who may include the attorney) on specific occasions (see below).

Remember that an attorney must act with 'utmost good faith' (see Chapter 10). Apart from these exceptions, the attorney should not 'dip into your cookie jar' for themselves.

In practice, an unscrupulous attorney will be able to abuse their position because they will have total control, with minimal supervision, at a time when you are at your most vulnerable. This is one of the reasons why you should choose your attorneys with, according to our own phrase, 'utmost good care' (see Chapter 9).

Can my attorney use my assets to make gifts?

Yes, they can, unless you make a restriction in your enduring power of attorney, *but there are limits*. Your attorney can make gifts of a seasonal nature (Christmas, weddings, anniversaries, birthdays, etc) which you yourself would normally give. These must be reasonable in amount in relation to your net worth – a £10,000 birthday gift from a £20,000 estate would not be reasonable!

The attorney can also make provision for dependants to the same extent as you might.

If the attorney wants to make more substantial gifts, for example, as part of a tax-saving strategy, they should take legal advice. The answer might be to apply to the Court of Protection for permission to make the gift. Care must be taken in considering the implications for the donor's will.

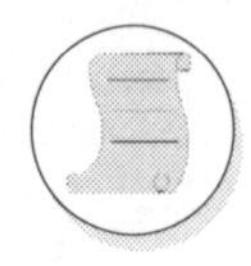

The whole question of what gifts are and are not allowable under an EPA was considered in the case of *Phillips v Cameron* in 1999. A rich old lady, Mrs Cameron, had three prudent sons and one improvident one, Donald, whose wife had divorced him and taken their son, Jamie, with her. Old Mrs Cameron conferred an EPA on the three prudent sons, helped by their solicitor, Mr Phillips. When she lost mental capacity the EPA was registered and her attorneys managed her affairs. To comply with what the old lady would have wanted, and also to save Inheritance Tax, they used her assets to set up trust funds to educate all her grandchildren, including Jamie. These gifts to the grandchildren would be deducted from their respective fathers' inheritances. Donald was not consulted and did not know about Jamie's trust fund. It was only after Mrs Cameron died that Donald found out that his inheritance had been depleted to provide for Jamie's education. He went to court, alleging that the attorneys had exceeded their powers.

He lost his case: the judge decided that an attorney could only make gifts or provide for dependants within the limits of the legislation, but he was generous in his interpretation. What had really caused the problem was how the gift made by the attorney affected the interpretation of the donor's will, and the distribution of her estate, after she died.

My elderly mother's mental capacity comes and goes. Is it too late for her to grant me an EPA? What is the minimum mental capacity required?

The **Public Guardianship Office** (PGO) says that the legal test (established in two landmark cases in 1988, *Re F* and *Re K*) is whether your mother can understand that:

- the attorney will have complete control over her affairs if she becomes mentally unable to manage them herself;
- the attorney will, in general, be able to do anything with her assets that she could have done;

- the power will continue if she becomes mentally incapable;
- if she does become mentally incapable, the power will become irrevocable (set in stone!) unless the **Court of Protection** steps in.

It is sufficient that your mother understands these points in a lucid interval. If you think that the EPA may be challenged, it is sensible to get a doctor to witness your mother signing and for the doctor to provide a letter saying that she had sufficient **mental capacity** at the time. The doctor should assess your mother's mental capacity by asking specific questions to establish her understanding of the issues. The doctor will almost certainly expect a fee for this.

I am an executor of my late sister's estate. I have a grant of probate, but the administration is a lot more complicated than I expected. Can my attorney handle this for me if I lose mental capacity?

No.

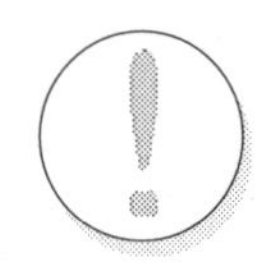

I am an executor of my late sister's estate. I do not have a grant of probate yet. Can I ask my attorney to take over?

Maybe – the rules are complex. Take professional advice.

I am the co-owner of our home with my spouse. If I grant my spouse an EPA, will they be able to sell our home after the EPA is registered?

Yes, but not on their own, because of the '**two trustee rule**'. The commonest situation where the two trustee rule applies is in situations like yours, where the family home is in the name of two spouses or partners. As the law sees it, they are both trustees and both must therefore sign any transfer documents, etc. If one partner grants the other an EPA, the attorney cannot on their own sign a transfer of property. The solution is simple: the attorney appoints a second trustee, who could be the solicitor handling the transaction. The attorney must also, within three months of the transaction, provide a statement that the **donor** is co-owner of the property.

I am a trustee of a small family trust for my young grandchildren. The trust fund is made up of investments, mainly shares, which we shall want to sell. Can my attorney under an EPA do this for me?

Yes, but only if the EPA complies with section 25 of the Trustee Act 1925 (as amended by the Trustee Delegation Act 1999). The requirements are that the power relates to a specific trust, lasts for no more than 12 months, notice of the power is given to all other trustees, and the **statutory** wording is used. If this bothers you (and we are sure it will), please take professional advice.

There is an obvious problem – what happens after the 12 months (see above) expires? A less obvious problem is posed by the **two trustee rule**. If the attorney is the other trustee, the law does not allow the attorney to appoint another trustee where the trust asset is something other than real estate.

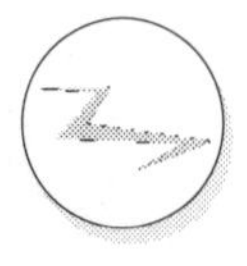

In practice, trustees should avoid long-term use of power of attorney. The easy fix is to appoint one or more extra trustees and put the trust assets into their names.

Take legal advice.

I am a trustee of the village playgroup. Can my attorney under an EPA continue to do this for me?

The answer is the same as for the small family trust, above.

How does my attorney sign documents? Do they use my name or theirs?

The law seems to permit them to use either. In practice – use both – for example, 'Mark Fairweather as attorney for Rosy Border'.

Can a body, such as a bank, be an attorney?

Yes. They cannot *grant* EPAs, but they can *be granted* them. There are advantages of continuity in appointing your bank. Banks don't, in general, die, emigrate or decide that being your attorney is just too much trouble. On the other hand, there are two disadvantages:

- their service is likely to lack the personal touch;
- it will cost you!

I have a joint bank account with my wife. What will happen to the account if I become mentally incapable?

Most joint personal accounts are set up so as to operate on a single signature, so the bank will not know unless your wife tells them. If and when she does so, the original signing mandate which allows either of you to sign cheques, etc, will be revoked. This will freeze the account, but most banks look at each individual case on its merits and will be sympathetic about payment of essential bills, such as utilities, until things have been sorted out.

If you have not signed an EPA, your wife will not be able to operate the account after you lose mental capacity, even though the bank mandate allows single signatures on cheques. She will need to apply to the PGO for appointment as your **receiver**.

If you have signed an EPA, your **attorney** (whether this is your wife or someone else) will be able to reactivate the account, although the bank may not allow this until after the EPA has been registered. The bank will, as a matter of practice, also normally prefer to close the joint account and operate separate sole accounts. There is a presumption that the money will be split 50/50, but this would not always apply (see Chapter 10).

I am my husband's second wife. We live on his work pension. He has signed an EPA appointing his son by his first marriage as his attorney. My husband is becoming mentally incapable. The son dislikes me and says that he has no intention of letting me have a penny of his father's pension after he takes over. Can he do this?

He might try. Get in first, if you can! If your husband still has mental capacity, ask him to sign a new EPA with a specific instruction that the attorney is to provide for you. You could also ask him to make you an attorney along with his son. See a solicitor about this to prevent allegations of undue influence. If it is too late for a new EPA, you can seek to pre-empt your stepson

- by objecting to the registration of the EPA on the grounds that the son is unsuitable (although he might claim that he is acting in his father's best interests, an attorney has the power to provide for the **donor**'s dependants to the same extent as the donor would), *or*
- by contacting the pension trustees *now* and telling them what is happening. They may have the discretion to pay at least part of the pension direct to you. Some do.

Can I grant my elderly sister an enduring power of attorney, with powers to appoint someone of her choice as her successor if she is unable to act for me?

No. If you did that your EPA would not be valid.

What you could do is set up two EPAs – one with your sister as your attorney, the other appointing someone else – *whom you must name* – to act for you if your sister is unable to do so. The PGO themselves make this point in their helpful booklet, *Enduring Power of Attorney – A Guide to Making an Enduring Power of Attorney or Taking on the Role of Attorney* (see 'Useful contacts').

I have arthritis in my hands and cannot sign anything properly. I use a rubber stamp for my cheques, with my bank's co-operation. How do I sign my Enduring Power of Attorney?

Have no fear! There is provision for this: see 'Suppose you can't write' on p 100.

Can my attorney consent to medical treatment on my behalf?

No. Your attorney has no power to do this. If, at the time the need for treatment arises, you still have **mental capacity**, you will be able to consent to or refuse treatment in your own right.

If you do not have mental capacity at the time you need medical treatment, the medical team will make a decision in what they consider to be your best interests after consultation with your family. Consider making a **living will** to make your views known in advance. Read Part 1 of this book and weigh up the pros and cons of doing this.

Can I alter the standard EPA form to suit my own requirements?

No. It is a **statutory** form. What you can do is limit or clarify the powers you give your attorney. We show you how in Chapter 11. Even the explanatory information and the notes are part of the form – so don't delete them by mistake – or, even worse, on purpose!

I am considering appointing my solicitor as my attorney, but what if she leaves the firm or dies in the meantime?

An EPA which allows the attorney to appoint a successor will be invalid. Furthermore, the attorney must be a named individual over 18 who is not bankrupt, or a special form of company known as a trust corporation. This appears to rule out a 'generic' appointment such as 'the senior partner in the firm of Stoat, Ferret and Weasel solicitors' – this is, at least, the view of the PGO. So the resignation, incapacity, bankruptcy or death of your solicitor would terminate your EPA. If this concerns you, consider appointing a bank or other trust corporation as your attorney (though it will cost you).

Can my attorney have my poor old dog put down?

A lot depends on the reasons why this might be necessary. Is the dog costing a fortune in vet bills, a fortune you cannot afford? Or are you going into a home where the dog is not allowed? Or do you no longer recognise the dog? In these situations, yes – the attorney can have your dog put down, after taking your needs and wishes into account.

Is an EPA just for old people?

No, there is no age limit – upper or lower – for adults, although older people are clearly more at risk of losing mental capacity. There is some doubt among lawyers as to whether anyone under the age of 18 can grant an EPA.

So, can any adult grant an EPA?

Yes, with the following exceptions.

- Someone suffering from mental illness might be able to grant an EPA in a lucid spell, but would usually be said to lack the **mental capacity** to grant one.
- An EPA signed under the influence of drink would be ineffective. One has visions of a drunken sailor waking up with a sore head, a tattoo and an EPA. If, however, at the time of granting it, you were so inebriated that you did not know what you were doing, the EPA – unlike your tattoo – would be void or, at the least, voidable. We are not expecting many drunken sailors to read this. If it applies to you, please cancel what you did – and start again.

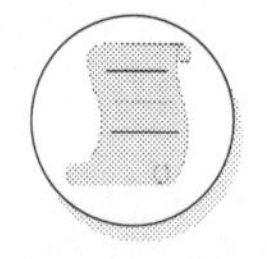

An 'enemy alien' – that is, someone who lives or conducts business in an enemy state in times of war – cannot grant an enduring power of attorney for someone to act for them in the UK. Interestingly, however, an expatriate enemy alien – a citizen of an enemy state who does not live or work there – can grant an EPA. We are not sure who, if anyone, would count as an enemy alien at the time of writing ...

Will the staff at the Public Guardianship Office (PGO) advise me about granting an EPA?

No. If you need help, take professional advice from a solicitor.

Can I set limits on my attorneys' powers?

Yes. See below.

I have three sons and I do not want to favour one over the others. Can I appoint more than one attorney?

Yes. You can, within reason, have as many attorneys as you like, and you are free to appoint your three sons jointly. Think carefully, however: do you want them to have a *joint* power or a *joint and several* power?

With a *joint* power, they must make any decisions *unanimously*; a decision by just one attorney would not be binding. Furthermore, if one joint attorney died, the enduring power of attorney would be cancelled.

With a *joint and several* power, decisions do not have to be unanimous and the enduring power of attorney would continue even if one or more attorney died (see p 87).

I am 89 and physically frail. My affairs are very simple. I do not own my own home and have very little in the bank. The only income I have is from state benefits. Do I need an EPA?

No, there is no legal requirement. An **agent** can collect your benefits for you. If you lose **mental capacity**, an **appointee** can take responsibility for claiming your benefits.

It would still, however, be preferable to appoint an **attorney** under an EPA so that they can get at the money in your bank account. This is because if you lose mental capacity your account will be frozen. The alternative to an EPA is the appointment of a **receiver**, but from what you say about your affairs, the costs of this exercise may well wipe out your savings.

Is an EPA valid if it is signed under duress?

No. An EPA signed under duress will not be valid. The same applies to:

- 'undue influence' (such as when a son or daughter pushes hard to get you to grant them an EPA but stops short of actually tying you up or threatening you with violence);
- fraud – where the potential attorney pretends, for example, that the document you are signing is something different.

When my attorneys register my EPA with the Public Guardianship Office, will they need to produce evidence that I have lost mental capacity?

Not unless the EPA itself contains a condition that requires this. In general, if the attorneys are in any doubt they should get a professional opinion before registering.

When my attorneys register my EPA, do they have to notify me that they are doing so?

Yes. You must be given notice of your attorneys' intention on a special form, EP1, and this form must be *given to you personally* (even if you do not understand what is going on). If this would cause you harm or distress, the PGO can dispense with this requirement but will expect evidence, such as a letter from your doctor (see p 104).

Who else does my attorney have to tell when they apply to register the Enduring Power of Attorney?

As well as yourself, at least three of your relatives, if possible. These notices are also sent out using form EP1, but they do not have to be served personally (post is sufficient). The people to be notified are listed on p 105. Of course, if you have fewer than three relatives, your attorney will have to tell the PGO – there is another special form for this.

How can anybody find out whether an EPA has been registered for a mentally incompetent person, and who their attorney is?

By asking the PGO to do a search. The fee for this is £20 (as of September 2003) and they must apply on form EP4 to:

> The Enduring Power of Attorney Team
> The Public Guardianship Office
> Archway Tower
> 2 Junction Road
> London N19 5SZ
> EPA help line: 0845 330 2963

You can download form EP4 from the PGO's website: www.guardianship.gov.uk.

Until the EPA is registered this is, of course, a private matter.

Why would anyone want to do that?

Family politics. Need we say more?

When does an enduring power of attorney end?

If and when *you*

- cancel it while you still have **mental capacity**, and cancel it properly (see p 109); *or*
- die; *or*

in the case a *sole* or *joint* (*not* **joint and several**, see above) attorney, *your attorney*

- resigns (as long as they do it properly – see p 109);
- dies; *or*
- becomes mentally incapable (if they become physically incapable, they should follow the procedure for resigning);
- goes bankrupt (see p 86).

In the case of a **joint and several** power of attorney, the remaining attorney can continue to act for you.

An EPA will also come to an end if

- you grant it for a fixed period of time, and that time expires;

- your attorney applies to register the EPA but the application is refused;
- the **Court of Protection** cancels the EPA, for whatever reason, after registration.

Will my attorney have any say over where I am to live?

In theory, no. Attorneys have control over your finances, but not 'power over the person'.

In practice, your finances may well be a crucial factor in deciding where you will live. To the extent that your attorney controls your finances, they will have a significant say in where you live if this is a decision that you are unable to take for yourself.

The PGO says: 'Power over the person and financial matters are often inextricably intertwined: the donor cannot stay put if there is no money for this, or if staying put is not in their best interests. The donor's wishes must be taken into account, as well as expert opinions (eg doctors, social workers) and other family members.'

Can my attorney make a will on my behalf?

No – but read on; all may not be lost. To make a will you need 'testamentary capacity' – that is, sufficient mental competence for that task. It is plainly sensible to make your will while you still have testamentary capacity – see *Wills and Estate Planning* in the *Pocket Lawyer* series.

If you have not made a will while you still have the **mental capacity** to do so, your attorney cannot write one for you, but they (and others closely affected) can apply to the **Court of Protection** for a **statutory will** (see also 'Wills', p 94).

Can my attorney insist on my solicitor letting them see my will?

If you still have **mental capacity**, only if you instruct your solicitor to that effect. The solicitor can only act on your instructions.

If at the time you no longer have mental capacity, your solicitor should, strictly speaking, ask the PGO – unless the EPA itself allows disclosure.

You should consider whether your EPA should contain the power to disclose the contents of your will. Otherwise, for example, your attorney may, in all innocence, sell an asset which you intend to leave to someone in your will.

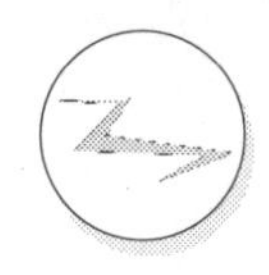

What will happen if I do become mentally incapable after granting an EPA, but my attorney does not apply to register the EPA with the Public Guardianship Office?

The power is not revoked by your mental incapacity (that is the whole point of an EPA), but your attorney's authority is severely limited – in effect, suspended – until the EPA has been registered. The PGO says that during this 'interregnum' (period in between), the attorney's powers are limited to:

- maintaining you;
- preserving your assets and property.

Are there any time limits for applying to register an EPA?

Yes. Your attorney must apply to register your EPA within 10 days of giving notice of their intention to do so to you and to your relatives (see Chapter 5). There is, however, no time limit as such for starting this procedure, although the PGO suggest that it is done sooner rather than later, because otherwise your attorney's authority will be severely limited (see above).

Can my attorney apply to register my EPA before I lose mental capacity?

Yes. They can make the application if you are, *or are becoming*, mentally incapable. The purpose of this provision is to enable your attorney to step in before your affairs get into a complete mess – not to put you away because you can't finish today's *Times* crossword!

I am the attorney of someone who has a substantial portfolio of shares. Can I vote on their behalf at shareholders' meetings?

Yes – but you will have to do so as a 'proxy'. Apply to the company well before the meeting for a proxy form and supply them with a copy of the EPA.

Does the law of EPAs apply outside England and Wales?

No. The PGO says: 'You do not have to live in England or Wales, but unless you have assets there, there may not be a need to appoint an attorney.' Scotland has Continuing Powers of Attorney, which are similar (see 'Useful contacts').

Powers of attorney

An **enduring power of attorney** (which we will refer to from now on as an EPA) is just one of several types of power of attorney. Any power of attorney is an authority granted by **deed** to act on behalf of someone else in respect of their property and financial affairs. The person who gives that power is called variously the **donor**, **grantor** or principal, and the person who is given the power is called the **attorney** or **donee**.

Your attorney is your agent, but a special agent (without, however, a licence to kill!). This is because:

- Your attorney has a clear *written* mandate in a standard format. The scope – and limitations – of your attorney's power should be clear. By contrast, one of the problems that agents (and people dealing with them) have in practice is not knowing if they are overstepping the mark.
- Your attorney has authority to carry out certain transactions which an ordinary agent cannot do – specifically transactions which require a deed, such as dealings with real estate.
- Your attorney has a document of appointment which people dealing with the attorney will recognise as valid. This is particularly helpful to the attorney, for example in dealing with government authorities and banks. The attorney can brandish the document, and as with a magic wand, doors will open. And the document is useful for people dealing with the agent: they know that they can rely on the document as proof of the appointment and the power that it confers. An agent can also be appointed in writing as well, but there is no standard wording – and as a result in many situations the magic effect just isn't there.

You can set the limits on your attorney's authority over your property and financial affairs, but in any case the authority cannot confer 'power over the person'. So, for example, your attorney cannot – in theory at least – make decisions about:

- how you live your life;
- your medical treatment; or
- where you are to live.

In practice, of course, these decisions are intertwined with your financial affairs and the limits on your attorney's authority may be less clear cut than you might imagine. (The King Lear scenario: the poor old buffer thought he was handing over his business affairs and then found his lifestyle severely cramped.)

Furthermore, things your attorney *cannot* take on for you include:

- writing your will;
- acting as a director of a company on your behalf – although the rules of most companies allow a director to appoint an 'alternate', and this could be (but need not be) your attorney. Moreover, if you lose **mental capacity**, most companies have rules which automatically bar you from continuing as a director;
- taking over from you as an executor of the estate of someone who has died, after you have obtained probate;
- taking over from you as trustee, unless you comply with specific **statutory** requirements.

Subject to these restrictions, it is up to you to specify exactly what powers you wish to give your attorney. A useful distinction is between a *general* power of attorney and a *limited* one.

A *general* power of attorney will empower the attorney to do anything in respect of your property and affairs which you could lawfully have done yourself. Your attorney could, for example, operate your bank account, manage your properties, run your business, sell your house and invest money on your behalf.

A *limited* power of attorney will give your attorney the power only to deal with one or more particular matter(s), such as selling your house.

You can also give someone a power of attorney (either general or limited) for a set period of time, such as while you are working abroad. Equally well, you can appoint an attorney for an indefinite period.

An enduring power of attorney

Subject to a couple of unusual exceptions, all appointments of **agents** and attorneys other than by EPA are automatically cancelled if the **donor** becomes mentally incapable. The main exception is what is called an *irrevocable* power of attorney. This is a special form of power which is often found in mortgages, and gives the lender power to do things in the borrower's name if the borrower defaults on the repayments. In order to protect the lender's position, the power will continue in force until hell freezes over. In fact, an irrevocable power can arise only in this type of situation – where the power is coupled with an interest. The other exception is where no one actually knows that the **donor** has lost their **mental capacity**.

There is a way around this problem, however, which is to confer a power of attorney which is *not* cancelled if and when you lose your mental capacity. This is to grant an EPA: an *enduring power of attorney*, which does what its name suggests – it *endures*. It carries on even after you, the **donor**, have become mentally incapable of handling your own affairs.

An EPA is, therefore, an important safeguard for people who are vulnerable to mental incapacity. Those most likely to benefit are the elderly, but it is worth bearing in mind that mental incapacity is only a road accident away even for the young and healthy.

An EPA goes on and on

An EPA continues until *you*:

- cancel it – while you still have **mental capacity**, and do so properly (see p 109); *or*
- go bankrupt; *or*
- die.

Or, in the case of a *sole* or *joint* (*not* **joint and several**, see above) attorney, your EPA carries on until *your attorney*:

- resigns (as long as they do it properly;
- dies;
- becomes mentally incapable (if they become physically incapable, they should follow the procedure to resign);
- goes bankrupt (see p 86).

In the case of a **joint and several** power of attorney, the remaining attorney can continue to act for you even if one or more of the others drops out for any reason.

An EPA will also come to an end if:

- you grant it for a fixed period of time, and that time expires;
- your attorney applies to register the EPA but the application is refused;
- the **Court of Protection** cancels the EPA, for whatever reason, after registration.

If you do not grant an enduring power of attorney

The world will not end if you lose **mental capacity**, but an EPA is almost invariably more convenient than the other options available to your family, as outlined here.

Soldier on

If your only income is your state benefits, a close relative or friend can apply to become what is known as an **appointee** to claim and deal with your state benefits for you.

An *appointee* can arrange for your benefits to be paid in cash at the post office or direct into *their* bank account, although, of course, the money must be used for *your* needs. This is particularly useful where a bank account cannot be operated in your own name because you have lost mental capacity.

For further information, see Social Security leaflet GL21, *A Helping Hand for Benefits?* This is available from social security offices, Citizens Advice Bureaux and online at www.ssani.gov.uk/forms_leaflets/general/GL21.pdf.

In the meantime, if you are physically frail but mentally alert, you can

- appoint an **agent** to collect your state benefits for you;
- write a letter of authority to your bank to allow someone else to sign cheques for you; or

- put your money into a joint account for the same purpose.

Remember, however, that if and when the bank learns that you have lost **mental capacity**, the authority to the bank and/or the joint account will be frozen.

Apply to the Public Guardianship Office (PGO) for the Court of Protection to appoint someone to manage your affairs

Application packs are available from the customer services helpline, tel 0845 3302900; or access www.guardianship.gov.uk to download the forms.

There is an application fee of £65 (waived in cases of genuine need; call the PGO helpline for details) and a lot of form-filling:

- Receiver's Declaration;
- Medical Certificate;
- Statement of Client's Assets and Income; and
- Notification Letter.

Everything is explained in *Protection*, a leaflet available on the website at www.guardianship.gov.uk/Protection.html or by post via the helpline (see 'Useful contacts'). There is also a helpful booklet, *Making an Application*, which you can order from the customer services helpline or download from the PGO website. (Even so, Rosy, who loathes filling in forms, found the Application Pack very daunting – the Statement of Client's Assets and Income alone runs to 32 pages!)

What the PGO will do then will depend on how much money and/or property you have. They can:

- **make a *short order***

  If you have capital of less than £16,000 and there is no property to be sold, the court will normally make a **short order**. A short order authorises someone – usually a family member – to:

  - receive pensions and trust income;
  - receive all or part of the money in your bank or building society accounts;

- pay nursing home fees or other charges, debts, legal costs, etc;
- provide for the safe custody of documents (such as your will), valuables, etc.

- **appoint a receiver**

  If your assets come to more than £16,000, the court will appoint a **receiver**. This is someone who has authority to look after the affairs of someone who is mentally incapable of doing so for themselves (the PGO's word for this person is *client*). The receiver can be anyone: a relative, a friend, a professional such as a solicitor, an accountant or an officer from the local authority. The person who makes the application can ask to be appointed, or nominate somebody else. In practice, receivers are usually family members. If nobody is available, or if there is a dispute, the court may consider appointing a receiver from their approved panel of professionals. They will, of course, expect to be paid.

Once appointed, the receiver has a duty to manage your financial affairs. This may include:

- receiving all or part of your money held in bank or building society accounts;
- paying any medical, legal, nursing home fees, etc;
- paying your debts or the receiver's own out-of-pocket expenses;
- selling your property or land, or ending a tenancy;
- disposing of your furniture or household effects;
- providing accounts to show how they have dealt with your money;
- carrying out any other actions in your best interests;
- making sure documents such as your will or share certificates are kept safely.

Handling someone's affairs is a big responsibility and all receivers are required to take out a type of insurance called a *security bond*. This is to cover any loss to the client if the receiver fails to carry out their responsibilities.

How much insurance the receiver will have to take out depends on how much of your money they can expect to handle each year. The sum insured will be the same as *either*

- your yearly income, *or*
- your yearly spending,

whichever is higher, plus a 'cushion' of about 50%. The minimum sum insured would be £5,000, rising in steps of £2,500. Additionally, the PGO will require:

- an appointment fee of £500 (when the receiver is first appointed);
- an annual administration fee – currently £205;
- a winding-up fee of £360 when you die.

There are additional fees for various transactions. A leaflet is available: *Our Fees and Charges*. Call the helpline for a copy, or visit the website given on p 80.

Note that the receiver does not pay out personally; it all comes out of *your* assets. The start-up and running costs (and mopping-up costs) of a receiver are likely to be significantly higher than those of an **attorney**.

There are, however, practical advantages in granting an EPA while you still have **mental capacity**:

- Your **attorney** will have a document to prove they are acting for you.
- Your attorney will have authority to operate your bank account even if you lose mental capacity.
- If you have shares or other investments, an attorney will be able to buy and sell them on your behalf.
- The concept of agency is a familiar and important one in the commercial world. If, however, you appoint an agent to deal with your private affairs, people are likely to be unwilling to deal with your agent – even if strictly speaking the appointment of an agent is all that the situation requires.
- The Inland Revenue's view is that tax returns must be signed personally by the taxpayer unless they are unable to do so, in which case an attorney or a receiver can sign (an agent won't do).
- Although a receivership would offer the same benefits as those mentioned above, an EPA is something you can organise for yourself, in your own way, while you still have mental capacity.
- An EPA is also cheaper, quicker (although in an emergency, a potential receiver can ask for an interim order to tide them over) and less bureaucratic than a receivership.

Choosing your attorney(s)

Let us assume that you have decided to consider granting someone an enduring power of attorney (EPA). Before you set about choosing your attorney(s), think about the job description.

Remember that your attorney will have access to all your money, business affairs and property at a time when you do not know what is going on.

To spell it out, an attorney with full powers will be able to:

- move money in and out of your bank account;
- do the same with your savings accounts;
- manage your business, with all that this entails;
- buy and sell goods on your behalf;
- buy and sell shares on your behalf;
- buy and sell property on your behalf;
- make certain gifts (see p 93) on your behalf.

Whatever else you do, do not appoint an attorney who might abuse the power they will have over you at a time when you are at your most vulnerable. The Master of the Court of Protection, Denzil Lush, estimates that 10–15% of registered attorneys of EPAs abuse their position for personal gain. He suspects the scale of abuse is even higher among unregistered attorneys. It is clearly better not to appoint an attorney at all than to risk this happening.

You will want to choose someone who understands you and is in tune with your way of thinking; someone who will use your money wisely. Your attorney will need to be a very special person. The mnemonic is **ATTORNEY**.

A ccessible – for most purposes, it's helpful if your attorney is no more than a reasonable distance away. Try not to choose someone who lives 200 miles away, or someone who may be backpacking in Nepal when you need them most.

T ime – you don't want an attorney who is too busy to do the job.

T rustworthy – your attorney must be someone with total integrity who will carry out the task with 'utmost good faith'– this is non-negotiable.

O rganised – your attorney will have to keep good records of transactions for the **Public Guardianship Office** (PGO) as well as the Inland Revenue.

R eliable – you don't want an attorney who will give up the job if the going gets tough.

N ous – your attorney needs to be reasonably streetwise in financial matters, and have the sense to take professional advice when they need it.

E mpathy – it is preferable to have someone who is in tune with your way of thinking and who will use your money as you would like it used.

Y outh – well, this is relative, but you want someone who will at least outlive you! As you may want someone with a longer shelf life than a member of your own generation, consider appointing a son, daughter, nephew or niece. Of course, the attorney must be over the age of 18, as minors (people under 18 years of age) cannot make valid contracts.

Other considerations are: **do you want a family member or a professional?**

Family members will generally be more accessible and less expensive than professionals, but will they do such a good job? A family attorney must apply *the same skill and care in administering your affairs as they would if they were handling their own affairs*. Ask yourself how well your potential attorney handles their own finances!

An attorney who is, for example, an accountant or a solicitor must apply *a professional standard of skill and care.* Whilst a professional attorney will charge for their services, family members will usually want their expenses paid and, for better or worse, they sometimes develop a sense that your assets owe them a living. The temptation to help themselves may be irresistible, particularly for family attorneys who are themselves strapped for cash. Believe us on this one!

Also, there are other reasons why a professional attorney may be the best option:

- a family attorney is not under a contractual duty to act, and can therefore give themselves an easy ride. A professional attorney will have a contractual duty to you and, very possibly, a duty of care to your family, so they cannot skimp the work they do on your behalf without making themselves liable for the consequences;
- all attorneys are expected to keep accounts, but those maintained by solicitors and qualified accountants must comply with the accounting rules of their own professions;
- if you have a lot of money and/or property, consider whether a 'lay' attorney would be able to handle your affairs as effectively as a professional would, and also whether it is fair to expect this of them – horses for courses.

Do you want one attorney or more than one?

You can get by with just one attorney. Remember, however, that if your only attorney dies or withdraws from the arrangement for whatever reason (see p 77), your EPA will automatically be cancelled. The same thing will happen if you have two *joint* attorneys – see below. If, however, you have more than one attorney with **joint and several** powers, the death or withdrawal of one attorney will not cancel the power and the remaining attorney can continue to act for you. Another advantage of multiple attorneys is that they can keep an eye on each other.

Two useful tests are:

- Do I want this person to have their hands in my cookie jar?
- How efficiently do they handle their own affairs (see above)?

The following people are automatically disqualified:

- anyone under the age of 18 (no offence meant – it's just that they can't enter into a range of legally binding contracts);
- bankrupts – it isn't just the temptation; they are actually legally barred from being your attorney under an EPA (but, interestingly, not from being an ordinary power of attorney). Someone who has entered into an Individual Voluntary Arrangement (a form of private bankruptcy) must also be considered doubtful, at the very least;
- mentally incapable or disordered people. (Although the law does not explicitly disqualify such people from being appointed attorneys, the effect of the legislation appears to be that the appointment is followed by instant revocation).

Joint powers or *joint and several* powers?

If you appoint more than one attorney, you have to state on the form (see Chapter 11 and the website accompanying this book for an example) whether they are to have *joint* powers, or *joint and several* powers.

Joint powers

If the attorneys are to have *joint* powers, then they must act together, so in order to be binding, any decision they make must be unanimous.

Advantages:

- the joint attorneys police each other;
- as their decisions must be unanimous, it is more likely that they will think them over.

Disadvantages:

- if one dies or becomes bankrupt, or mentally incapable of performing their duties, or resigns, your EPA becomes ineffective;
- even the temporary absence or illness of one attorney will hold up business.

Joint and several powers

If your attorneys have *joint and several* powers, they can act and make decisions *either* together *or* separately.

Advantages:

- if one attorney dies or becomes bankrupt, or mentally incapable of performing their duties, or resigns, your EPA can still go on;
- if one attorney is temporarily absent or otherwise unavailable, business can continue as usual.

Disadvantages:

- one attorney could end up committing the other(s) to things they disagree with;
- joint and several powers dilute the control that the attorneys exert over each other.

There is a trap for the unwary here. If you have more than one attorney, the power must be either joint or *joint and several*. You cannot provide for majority decision-making (that is, two out of three won't do).

What powers should you give?

In most cases, there is probably little point in restricting your attorney's powers – but one instance might be an EPA which is intended to be *temporary*, such as to enable a **deed** to be signed while you are away on holiday. Otherwise, restrictions will simply make things difficult for your attorneys. If, however, you want to impose restrictions, you can

- limit the property and/or assets available to your attorneys, *and/or*

- limit what your attorneys can do with your property.

There are spaces on the EPA form for you to do this if you wish.

Although your attorney's primary duty will be to manage your affairs for your benefit, the attorney also has an implied power to benefit other people in the way you have in the past, or would in the future. This is particularly important where you have dependants – for example, if you have a spouse, partner, parent or children relying on your income. If you think that there might be doubt about the extent of your obligations, make the power into a duty by specifying in the EPA the people for whom the attorney is to make provision. We show you how on p 99.

Duties and rights of attorneys

Whether your attorney is a close friend or family member doing the job for expenses only, or a professional such as a solicitor charging for their work, they have the following duties.

- To act always with *utmost good faith* in their dealings with you. Your attorney's whole relationship with you is encapsulated in this one concept of 'utmost good faith'.

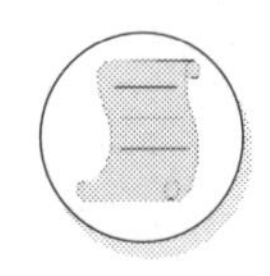

Many relationships involve good faith, But your attorney's relationship with you is one of 'utmost good faith – *uberrimae fidei*'. This demands the highest standard of integrity. Your attorney must put your interests first at all times. They must be not only clean, but squeaky clean.

- To register the Enduring Power of Attorney (EPA) as soon as they have reason to believe that your mental capacity is failing.
- To keep good accounts and records.

  An attorney who is a solicitor or a qualified accountant will, of course, be bound by their own professional accounting rules, but a lay attorney must also keep good accounts and records. Once your EPA has been registered, the **Court of Protection** can order your attorney to show them their records and accounts

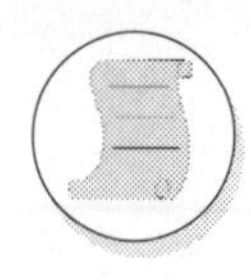

There is a strong incentive to keep accurate records. If your attorney mixes your property with theirs, by a famous court case (*Lupton v White* 1808) all the property will be said to belong to you and not to your attorney! Thus separate bank and building society accounts for donor and attorney are vital.

- Not to engage in transactions between themselves and you – 'internal' transactions – without revealing it beforehand. For example, they cannot buy your house for their own use without fully and fairly telling you (or the **Public Guardianship Office** (PGO) if the EPA has been registered) the precise terms of the deal. Strictly speaking, the attorney does not need your consent to the transaction because you have given them the powers to go through with it. All the same, if you object your attorney can hardly go through with the transaction without finding themselves in breach of their duty of *utmost good faith*. Where the EPA is registered, the attorney would be unwise to proceed without the court's prior consent.

If an attorney really wants to engage in an 'internal transaction', as well as disclosing their intentions they should also arrange for the **donor** of the power (you) to receive independent professional advice. If, by this stage, the EPA has been registered, the attorney should give the PGO independent valuations.

- Not to make 'secret profits' – for example, commissions for placing business.
- Not to exceed their authority as set out in the EPA. If you grant your attorney a limited power only, then your attorney must stay within the limits.
- To perform their duties with skill and care (see also p 84).

Taking stock – and taking action

Your attorney cannot do a good job of managing your affairs unless they know what is there to manage! They should start by taking stock – making an inventory of your assets and your liabilities, your income and your outgoings. A couple of spreadsheets will not come amiss – one to calculate a balance sheet of your assets less liabilities, the other to show a 'profit and loss account' of your income and outgoings.

Here is a checklist of possible assets:

- real estate (such as your home, land, etc) ❑
- contents ❑
- cars ❑
- bank and building society deposits ❑
- Premium Bonds and other forms of national savings ❑
- other investments, such as shares ❑
- life insurance policies ❑
- pensions ❑
- works of art and antiques ❑
- business assets ❑
- tools and machinery ❑
- jewellery ❑
- other
- .... ❑
- .... ❑
- .... ❑
- .... ❑

Typical liabilities might be:

- mortgages, loans and overdrafts
- hire purchase
- credit card debts
- catalogue debts
- other debts

Sources of income might include:

- pensions, etc
- interest on savings
- share dividends
- rents from property
- welfare benefits

Ongoing expenditure might include:

- mortgages and other loan payments
- rents
- utilities
- council tax
- care and nursing fees
- insurance premiums

This information will enable your attorney to take a global view of your affairs and, specifically, to:

- protect your assets – are they secure, and are they properly insured? (see below);
- prepare a budget of income and expenditure – and stick to it;
- prepare accounts of income and expenditure.

A conscientious attorney will – especially after the EPA has been registered – attend to all aspects of your financial affairs, including the following.

- **Insurances**:
    - *physical assets* (buildings, contents, valuables, cars). The attorney really needs to carry out an 'insurance audit', to check that your assets are adequately insured, and that premiums are paid promptly on the renewal dates;

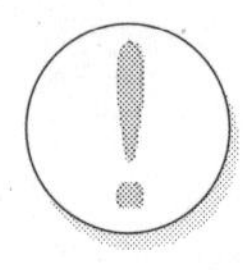

There is a trap with empty property. Most insurance policies lapse if the insured property is unoccupied for more than 28 days. In that event, your attorney must get in touch with the insurers, explain the situation and make sure that insurance cover will continue – either with the existing insurer or with another one who will accept the risk.

Similarly, if you move out of your home and let it instead, the insurers must be told, otherwise they may be able to avoid paying out on a claim.

- *life insurances* – it is *vital* to keep up the premium payments (and if you fall terminally ill your attorney may be able to claim on your behalf in advance of your death);
- *health insurances* (ditto);
- *car insurances* – if appropriate, notify the insurer of any additional drivers.

- **Pensions and welfare benefits** – your attorney should check that you are getting your full entitlements, including attendance allowance (which is not means-tested and does not necessarily involve having attendants: people living alone can qualify too).
- **Funding for residential and nursing care** – if you need to go into a care home and/or require nursing care, your attorney will have to get to grips with how this is to be paid for. This subject is outside the scope of this book, but 'Useful contacts' offers some good starting points.
- **Tax** – are you getting all your allowances? Remember that people aged 65–74, and people aged 75 and over, have age-related allowances. The Revenue's view is that tax returns must be signed by the taxpayer personally, although an exception is made for signatures by an attorney if the taxpayer is unable to sign for themselves (see 'Useful contacts' for details of the Revenue's informative website).
- **Bank accounts**. Your bank mandate will be cancelled as soon as the bank knows you have lost **mental capacity**, and this applies to joint accounts too. Your attorney will, however, be able to operate the account as soon as the EPA is registered. In practice, banks are often willing to release funds to pay essential bills such as utilities while waiting for the registration to go through. The bank will then usually want the funds transferred into a new account.

  In the case of a joint account, it is sensible to divide the money between the attorney and the other joint account holder and open two separate accounts. Otherwise, it is difficult for the attorney to keep track of the money and to ensure that the donor's money is used properly. There is a presumption that the money in a joint account is split 50/50, but this would not always apply if, for example, only one of the joint account holders has actually paid money into the account.
- **Family birthdays, anniversaries, etc**. Remember that the attorney can make gifts of a seasonal nature (Christmas, weddings, anniversaries, birthdays, etc) which you yourself would normally give. These

must be reasonable in amount in relation to your net worth – a £10,000 birthday gift from a £20,000 estate would not be reasonable!

Wills

Your attorney may want to check that you have made a will, although they will not be entitled to see the contents unless you specifically allow for this (see FAQ, p 72). However, it will often be sensible for you to let them see the contents of the will in order to avoid confusion. Otherwise, for example, an attorney who does not know what your intentions are in your will may, in all innocence, sell an asset that you intend to be given to someone when you die. We show you how to give your attorney authority to see your will on p 98.

If you have not made a will, and the intestacy rules (the rules which say who is to get what if you die without making a will) will produce an unwelcome result, your attorney, and others closely affected, can consider applying to the court for a **statutory will**. You can find out more about statutory wills from the Official Solicitor's website at www.offsol.demon.co.uk and also at www.guardianship.gov.uk.

If there is an urgent need for a statutory will, your attorney can ring the Court of Protection's Judicial Support Unit helpline, tel 020 7664 7178. In practice, your attorney should instruct a solicitor; statutory wills are not a DIY matter.

Of course, you can save everybody a lot of trouble and expense by making a will yourself, while you still have **mental capacity**. *Wills and Estate Planning* in the *Pocket Lawyer* series shows you how to do this.

Old Mrs Davey was rich – and senile. She had written a will leaving her estate to relatives. Her young male carer married her, and the marriage had the automatic effect of revoking her will and giving him the lion's share of her estate. The relatives applied for, and obtained, a *statutory will* reinstating the original will. Mr Gold-Digger got nothing.

Attorneys have rights too

Expenses – your attorney is entitled to reclaim their expenses, but to do so they should keep records and the expenses must be reasonable in amount and properly incurred. Expenses that can be reclaimed include travel and the cost of professional advice.

Remuneration – a professional attorney will almost invariably ensure that the EPA document includes a clause which allows them to charge for their services, including 'personal services' – not what you might think: these are services that do not require professional expertise but are still part of an attorney's duties.

There is no reason why you cannot enter into a contract with a family attorney to pay them in the same way (for further discussion of paying family attorneys, see FAQs, p 60).

After an EPA has been registered, an attorney can apply to the PGO for permission to charge for their services.

If you are not happy about paying a family member but would like them to have something in recognition of their time and effort, consider leaving them something in your will. This, in fact, may be more tax-efficient both for you and for your attorney, depending on your respective tax positions. For advice on this, see *Wills and Estate Planning* in the *Pocket Lawyer* series.

Completing and signing the enduring power of attorney form

(1) Rules is rules – in this case the Enduring Power of Attorney (Prescribed Form) Regulations 1990 (as amended) – phew! You *must* use the **statutory** form – a DIY version will not do.

Although you are not allowed the rewrite the form, you do have scope to add clauses that might be important to you. We show you the options.

You can obtain paper copies of the form from law stationers such as *Oyez* or *Stat Plus* for about £2 each. The one you can download from the *Oyez* website is wonderful, except that it has SPECIMEN printed across every page!

You can also order forms online from the HMSO website. An English version is at:

www.legislation.hmso.gov.uk/si/si1990/Uksi_19901376_en_1.htm

and a Welsh version is at:

www.legislation.hmso.gov.uk/si/si2000/20000289.htm

The form is contained in the Regulations and a fee (approximately £6) will be charged to have them posted to you by HMSO.

(2) You should read all of Part A of the form, or if you have difficulty reading, have it read out to you.

(3) You **must** complete Part B of the form, which you must sign in the presence of an independent, adult

witness, who should also give their name, address and occupation. Date Part B with the date of signing.

(4) *After* you have signed Part B, your attorney should sign Part C in the presence of a witness, as before. Use a separate Part C for each attorney – download spares from our website. Again, Part C should be dated with the date of actual signing.

Optional extra clauses

You don't *have to* add anything to the form, but here is a pick-and-mix selection of clauses that may suit your own circumstances. The place to put a clause of this sort is in Part B, under '*subject to the following restrictions and conditions*' (our comments follow each clause).

I wish my Attorney[s] to have access to my medical records. Production of this Power of Attorney will be sufficient authority for my doctors to release my medical records to my Attorney[s]

Medical records are, of course, confidential, but there may be times when it would be helpful for your attorney to have access to yours – for example, to establish whether you have **mental capacity**.

I wish my Attorney[s] to have access to my Will, which is held by [insert name and address]. Production of this Power of Attorney will be sufficient authority to release my Will to my Attorney[s]

If your will is held by your solicitor or bank, they will treat it as confidential unless they have a clear instruction otherwise. You may wish your attorney to have access to your will, for example, to prevent them from selling an asset that you wish to leave to someone.

Before applying to register my Enduring Power of Attorney, my attorney[s] shall obtain a certificate from a medical practitioner that I no longer have mental capacity to manage my affairs

There is no statutory requirement for your attorney to provide the PGO with medical evidence when applying for registration. You can, however, make this a condition.

My attorney[s] shall not act for me until they have reason to believe that I am, or am becoming, mentally incapable

Add the above wording if you want your attorney's powers to take effect only after you have lost mental capacity.

My attorney[s] shall make provision from my income and assets, to the same extent as I have in the past and/or would wish to in the future, for the following people [list names and addresses]

Your attorney has an implied power to make provision for dependants to the same extent as you have done in the past and would wish to do in the future. If you think the attorney might be in doubt, you can spell this out in this clause.

In addition to out of pocket expenses, my attorney[s] shall have the right to pay themselves reasonable and proper remuneration for their services as my attorney[s]

Your attorneys are entitled to reasonable expenses in any case, but you might wish to pay them for their trouble. This clause allows you to do so.

My attorney[s] shall keep full and accurate records of my income and expenditure, assets and liabilities. My attorney[s] shall prepare annual accounts, which they are to submit each year to [name and address of accountant, solicitor, etc] for approval

Your attorney[s] have an implied obligation to keep accounting records and prepare accounts and the PGO can demand to see them. In practice, the PGO is unlikely to do so unless someone tells them something is amiss. Consider requiring your attorney[s] to produce accounts annually to, for example, your solicitor or accountant.

Checklist

The PGO may well reject your EPA when your attorney applies for registration if you or your attorney(s) fill the form in incorrectly, so check the following:

Have you signed Part B before your attorney signed Part C? (You can both sign on the same day, but your attorney must not sign before you do.) ❑

Have you deleted either *jointly* or *jointly and severally*? ❑

Have you deleted *with general authority to act on my behalf* or *with authority to do the following on my behalf*? ❑

If you have deleted the *general authority*, have you spelt out exactly what you wish your attorney to do? ❑

Have you added any extra clauses you would like included (see above)? ❑

Suppose you can't write

If you made a previous EPA, have you cancelled this? If not, do so now. ❑

No problem. Someone else (not a witness to the signature or an attorney) can sign for you, but in this case there has to be a second witness. There is a space on the form. You need to add a statement on the form:

This form has been signed at my direction by

....

Where to keep your form

There is no legal requirement to do so, but it is sensible to give a copy of the form to each attorney with a note about where to find the original. This is because if you lose **mental capacity**, you may not remember where you put your EPA.

Important: keep the original somewhere safe, where it can easily be found if it is needed.

Registering your enduring power of attorney form

We all hope to die at an advanced age, in full possession of our faculties, but mental infirmity has no respect for our wishes and the day may come when you are no longer able to manage your own affairs. That is when the 'enduring' part of your Enduring Power of Attorney (EPA) kicks in.

The **Public Guardianship Office** (PGO) advises against registering at too late a stage and advocates approaching them 'sooner rather than later'. Mental deterioration can happen gradually and there may be plenty of warning that someone is losing their grip. When it is clear that your mental powers are failing, your attorney(s) must register your EPA with the **Court of Protection**.

To register your EPA, your attorney has to use a **statutory** form, EP2. *Nothing else will do* (see specimen EP2, p 113). At the time of writing, the fee for an application for an EPA to be registered is £220. This money is usually payable out of your assets. There is provision for the PGO to waive the fee if neither you nor your attorney can afford to pay.

Your attorneys do not need to include any evidence of your mental incapacity with their application unless you have specified in your EPA that they must do so. On the other hand, your attorneys may wish you to be seen by a doctor to satisfy themselves that they are doing the right thing in applying at this stage.

However, before they send in form EP2, your attorney has a **statutory** duty to let you and your family know what is happening.

Notification

The object of notification is, of course, to give you and your immediate family the opportunity to object if you or they disagree with the registration – for example, if you or they think that it is too early for your attorney(s) to take over the reins, or your family disapprove of your choice of attorney.

Rules is rules (again), and here they are.

- Your attorney must use the prescribed form – 'EP1 Notice of intention to apply for registration' (see specimen form EP1, p 111).
- The form must specify the names of all attorneys who wish their powers to be registered, and in the case of a *joint* power (see p 85) all attorneys must be named.
- All attorneys applying for registration must sign the form.
- If there are two or more attorneys and only one applies for registration, the other attorney(s) have to be notified. This is done on Form EP1.
- Notification must be given before your attorney applies for registration.
- The following people *must* be notified:

(1) You

Form EP1 must be *handed to you personally*, even if you do not understand what is going on.

If this would cause you harm or distress, the PGO can dispense with this requirement but it will expect evidence, such as a letter from your doctor.

Attorneys normally notify **donors** themselves. If for any reason someone other than your attorney does it, this fact must be stated on form EP2 (the form used for actually registering the EPA – see p 113 below), together with the name and address of the person who *did* notify you.

(2) Your relatives

Your attorney must now inform at least three of your relatives, if possible, using a separate form EP1 for each person. The forms do not have to be handed to them personally – first-class post will do.

Here are the categories of people to notify in order of precedence:

- your husband or wife;
- your children (this includes adopted children but not stepchildren);
- your parents;
- your brothers and sisters (this includes half-brothers and half-sisters);
- the widow or widower of any of your children who have died;
- your grandchildren;
- your nephews and nieces (that is, the children of your brothers and sisters);
- your aunts and uncles (but not those related to you only by marriage);
- your first cousins (that is, the children of your aunts and uncles).

Note that your attorney *does not* need to notify anyone:

- who is under the age of 18;
- who is mentally incompetent;
- whose address is not known (see below).

Moreover, your attorney is not under an obligation under the rules formally to notify unmarried partners/cohabitees. As a matter of good practice, you should, in our view, notify them anyway.

---

1 Consider stating in your EPA under 'Restrictions and Conditions' that application to register is not to be made until notification on form EP1 has been given to .... *(name the people)*. Alternatively, simply name them as an attorney in the first place.

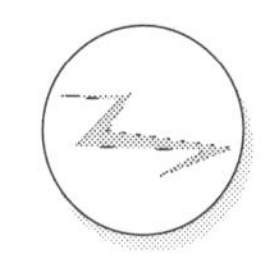

2 Leave an address list for your attorney and, if appropriate, state each person's relationship to you.

Here are further rules about notifying families:

- if your attorney is a notifiable relative, they can count themselves as having been notified;
- if you have fewer than three relatives, your attorney should notify whoever is available and state the circumstances on form EP2.
- if your attorney notifies one relative in a group they must notify them all (in other words, one cousin – all cousins), so they may end up serving far more than three EP1s to relatives.

All the notices must be sent out by first-class post, fax, document exchange or e-mail within 14 days of each other. The date of notification is deemed to be the date you *send* the notice and not the date it is *received*.

Your attorney must apply to register your EPA within 10 days of giving notice of their intention to do so to you and to your relatives on form EP1 (see above). There is no need for your attorney to wait for any objections. They can get on with applying for registration as soon as they have served (that is, sent) their EP1s.

Form EP2 – the application for registration

Your attorney must now send to the Public Guardianship Office (PGO) (see 'Useful contacts' for the address):

- Form EP2 (see specimen, p 113 and on our website);
- the original of your EPA form;
- a cheque for £220 made payable to 'Public Guardianship Office'.

If you have changed your address since filling in your original EPA form, your attorney will, of course, need to tell the PGO about this.

Registration is not immediate. The PGO will run a check to see that everything is in order, and the papers will be held for *35 days from the date of service* of the last form EP1. The purpose of this delay is to allow 28 days for potential objectors to get in touch before going through with the registration.

Then, if your attorney's paperwork is in order and nobody has lodged an objection, your EPA will be registered. The original document will be stamped with an official seal and returned to your attorney.

No refunds

If, for any reason, registration is refused, your attorney will not get their money back: the £220 is for the *application to register* your EPA, not for the registration itself. Let us hope, however, that all the paperwork will be in order and that nobody will object to registration.

Objections

You will see that form EP1 gives your relatives four weeks in which to object to the proposed registration of your EPA. Objectors must do so in writing to the PGO, not to your attorneys.

The possible grounds for objection are:

- that the EPA is not valid;
- that the power created by the instrument 'no longer subsists' (that is, has been revoked, or the attorney is dead/bankrupt/insane);
- that your attorneys have applied too early because you are not yet becoming mentally incapable;
- that fraud or undue pressure was used to make you grant your EPA;
- that the chosen attorney(s) is (are) unsuitable.

Objections must be in writing, and must include:

- the name and address of the person objecting;
- the name and address of the **donor** of the EPA,
- what relation (if any) the objector is to the donor;
- the attorney's name and address;
- the grounds for objecting to the EPA being registered.

What if someone does object?

There will be a court hearing and your attorney is likely to need professional advice.

In the interim – between application and registration

Between applying to register your EPA and getting its registration confirmed, your attorney cannot make any important decisions. Their powers are limited to (we quote the official leaflet) 'the maintenance of the Donor and preventing loss to the Donor's estate'.

After registration

Your attorney can manage your affairs, but they will still not have *carte blanche*. They have duties and responsibilities and must fulfil them (see Chapter 10). In practice, the court will not supervise your attorney too closely unless they have doubts about your attorney's actions.

Your attorney will need to liaise with your bank, building society, etc to inform them that your EPA has been registered.

Cancellation

That is, cancellation by you, the **donor**.

There are two steps to cancelling your EPA.

First, there must be an *act of cancellation*, preferably in writing. For example, you could write CANCELLED in large letters across each page of the original EPA and any copies you can get your hands on, and sign the cancellation.

Secondly, you must notify your soon-to-be-ex attorney – again preferably in writing – that the power is cancelled. Keep a copy of your letter. If you still have **mental capacity** but can no longer physically write, you can get someone else to do this for you.

Resignation

That is, resignation by an **attorney**.

Your attorney gives notice in writing that they no longer wish to act for you. The notice must be given:

- to you, if you have **mental capacity**; *or*
- to the PGO if you have lost or are losing mental capacity and, as a result, the attorney is under a duty to apply for registration; *or*
- to the Public Guardianship Office if your EPA has already been registered.

Note that if one *joint* attorney resigns, the EPA will be cancelled completely, but if one ***joint and several*** attorney pulls out, the EPA remains valid and the remaining attorney(s) can carry on.

As for **when** the disclaimer takes effect, it does so on the day you or the PGO receive it.

Divorce cancels an EPA

If you appoint your husband or wife as your attorney and you later divorce, you will need to make a new EPA.

A note on abuse

We have already mentioned that, according to the Master of the Court of Protection, up to 15% of registered attorneys abuse their powers. Most abuse takes the form of unlawful gifts. This is a despicable way to treat a frail and vulnerable person.

What should *you* do if you think this is happening to someone you know?

The short answer is, don't stand on the sidelines: blow the whistle at once. Get in touch with the EPA Team at the PGO (see 'Useful contacts') with as much evidence as you can gather. The Court of Protection can then order enquiries. If they are satisfied that there is substance to your allegations, they can cancel the power and order the rogue attorney to make amends.

Forms

Form EP1

SCHEDULE 1
Form EP1

Court of Protection
Enduring Powers of Attorney Act

Notice of intention to apply for registration

To...

Of...

This form may be adapted for use by three or more attorneys.

Give the name and address of the donor.

It will be necessary for you to produce evidence in support of your objection. If evidence is available please send it with your objection, the attorney(s) will be given an opportunity to respond to your objection.

The grounds upon which you can object are limited and are shown at 2 overleaf.

TAKE NOTICE THAT

I...

of...

and I...

of...

The attorney(s) of..

....

of...

....

intend to apply to the Court of Protection for registration of the enduring power of attorney appointing me (us) attorney(s) and made by the donor on the...

1. If you wish to object to the proposed registration you have 4 weeks from the day on which this notice is given to you to do so in writing. Any objections should be sent to the Court of Protection and should contain the following details:

- Your name and address
- Any relationship to the donor
- If you are not the donor, the name and address of the donor
- The name and address of the attorney
- The grounds for objecting to the registration of the enduring power

Note. The instrument means the enduring power of attorney made by the donor which it is sought to register.

2. The grounds on which you may object are:

- That the power purported to have been created by the instrument is not valid as an enduring power of attorney
- That the power created by the instrument no longer subsists.
- That the application is premature because the donor is not yet becoming mentally incapable.
- That fraud or undue pressure was used to induce the donor to make the power.
- That the attorney is unsuitable to be the donor's attorney (having regard to all the circumstances and in particular the attorney's relationship to or connection with the donor).

The attorney(s) does not have to be a relative. Relatives are not entitled to know of the existence of the enduring power of attorney prior to being given this notice.

Note. This is addressed only to the donor

3. You are informed that while the enduring power of attorney remains registered, you will not be able to revoke it until the Court of Protection confirms the revocation.

Note. This notice should be signed by every one of the attorneys who are applying to register the enduring power of attorney

Signed.....................................Dated.................

Signed.....................................Dated.................

Page 1 of 6

Form EP2

Court of Protection
Enduring Powers of Attorney Act 1985
Application for Registration

IMPORTANT: Please complete the form in BLOCK CAPITALS using a black ballpoint pen. For circled options please completely fill-in the appropriate choice.

Part One - The Donor

Please state the full name and present address of the donor. State the donor's first name in 'Forename 1' and the donor's other forenames/initials in 'Other Forenames'. If the donor's address on the enduring power of attorney is different give that one too. If necessary, complete several parts of the address on each Address line shown.

Mr ○ Mrs ○ Ms ○ Miss ○ Other ○ If Other, please specify here:

Last Name:

Forename 1:

Other Forenames:

Address 1:

Address 2:

Address 3:

Town/City:

County:

Postcode:

Address on the enduring power of attorney (if different from above) :

Address 1:

Address 2:

Town/City:

County: Postcode:

You can find the donor's date of birth in Part B of the enduring power of attorney.

Donor Date of Birth: D D M M Y Y Y Y

If the exact date is unknown please state the year of birth

Part Two - Attorney One

Please state the full name and present address of the attorney. If applicable, include the Company Name in 'Address 1'

Mr ○ Mrs ○ Ms ○ Miss ○ Other ○ If Other, please specify here:

Last Name:

Forename 1:

Other Forenames:

Continued overleaf

Part Two - Attorney One cont'd

Address 1:

Address 2:

Address 3:

Town/City:

County:

Postcode:

DX No. (solicitors only):

DX Exchange (solicitors only):

Attorney Date of Birth: D D M M Y Y Y Y

Occupation:

Daytime Tel No.: (STD Code):

Email Address:

Relationship to donor:

Spouse ○ Child ○ Other Relation ○ No Relation ○ Solicitor ○ Other Professional ○

If 'Other Relation' or 'Other Professional', specify relationship:

Part B of the enduring power of attorney states whether the attorney is to act jointly, jointly and severally, or alone.

Appointment *(please fill the appropriate circle)*: Jointly ○ Jointly and Severally ○ Alone ○

Part Three - Attorney Two

Please state the full name and present address of the second attorney. If applicable, include the Company Name in 'Address 1'.

Mr ○ Mrs ○ Ms ○ Miss ○ Other ○

If Other, please specify here:

Last Name:

Forename 1:

Other Forenames:

Address 1:

Address 2:

Address 3:

Town/City:

County:

Postcode:

DX No. (solicitors only):

DX Exchange (solicitors only):

Part Three - Attorney Two cont'd

Attorney Date of Birth: D D M M Y Y Y Y

Occupation:

Daytime Tel No.:

Email Address:

Relationship to donor:
Spouse ○ Child ○ Other Relation ○ No Relation ○ Solicitor ○ Other Professional ○

If 'Other Relation' or 'Other Professional', specify relationship:

Part Four - Attorney Three

Please state the full name and present address of the third attorney.
If applicable, include the Company Name in 'Address 1'.

Mr ○ Mrs ○ Ms ○ Miss ○ Other ○

If Other, please specify here:

Last Name:

Forename 1:

Other Forenames:

Address 1:

Address 2:

Address 3:

Town/City:

County:

Postcode:

DX No. (solicitors only):

DX Exchange (solicitors only):

Attorney Date of Birth: D D M M Y Y Y Y

Occupation:

Daytime Tel No.:

Email Address:

Relationship to donor:
Spouse ○ Child ○ Other Relation ○ No Relation ○ Solicitor ○ Other Professional ○

If 'Other Relation' or 'Other Professional', specify relationship:

If there are additional attorneys, please complete the above details in the 'Additional Information' section (at the end of this form).

Part Five - The Enduring Power of Attorney

The date is the date that the donor signed the enduring power of attorney.
You can find this in Part B of the enduring power of attorney.

I (We) the attorney(s) apply to register the enduring power of attorney made by the donor under the above Act, the original of which accompanies this application.
I (We) have reason to believe that the donor is or is becoming mentally incapable.

Date of enduring power of attorney: D D / M M / Y Y Y Y

To your knowledge, has the donor made any other enduring power of attorney?: Yes O No O

If 'Yes', please give details below including registration date if applicable:

Part Six - Notice of Application to Donor

Notice must be given personally to the donor. It should be made clear if someone other than the attorney(s) gives the notice.

I (We) have given notice of the application to register in the prescribed form (EP1) to the donor personally.

If someone other than the attorney gives notice to the donor please complete the name, address and date details below:

Full Name:
Address 1:
Address 2:
Town/City:
County: Postcode:

On this date: D D / M M / Y Y Y Y

Part Seven - Notice of Application to Relatives

If there are no relatives entitled to notice please ensure that the circle is filled below.

Please fill-in the circle if no relatives are entitled to notice: O

I (We) have given notice to register in the prescribed form (EP1) to the following relatives of the donor:

Name	Relationship to Donor	Address

Date notice given: D D / M M / Y Y Y Y

Name	Relationship to Donor	Address

Date notice given: D D / M M / Y Y Y Y

Name	Relationship to Donor	Address

Date notice given: D D / M M / Y Y Y Y

Name	Relationship to Donor	Address

Date notice given: D D / M M / Y Y Y Y

Continued overleaf

Part Seven - Notice of Application to Relatives cont'd

If there are additional relatives please complete the Relative Name, Relationship, Address and Date details in the 'Additional Information' section (at the end of this form).

Name	Relationship to Donor	Address

Date notice given:

D D M M Y Y Y Y

Part Eight - Notice of Application to Co-Attorney(s)

Do not complete this section if it does not apply. If there are additional co-attorneys please complete the Attorney Name, Relationship, Address and Date details in the 'Additional Information' section (at the end of this form).

Are all the attorneys applying to register? Yes ○ No ○

If no, I (We) have given notice to my (our) co-attorney(s) as follows:

Name	Relationship to Donor	Address

Date notice given:

D D M M Y Y Y Y

Name	Relationship to Donor	Address

Date notice given:

D D M M Y Y Y Y

Part Nine - Fees

Guidelines on remission postponement of fees can be obtained from the Court of Protection.

Have you enclosed a cheque for the registration fee for this application? Yes ○ No ○

Do you wish to apply for postponement or remission of the fee? Yes ○ No ○

If yes, please give details below:

Part Ten - Declaration

Note: The application should be signed by all attorneys who are making the application. This must not pre-date the date(s) when the notices were given.

I (We) certify that the above information is correct and that to the best of my (our) knowledge and belief I (We) have complied with the provisions of the Enduring Powers of Attorney Act 1985 and all of the Rules and Regulations.

Signed: Dated: D D M M Y Y Y Y

Signed: Dated: D D M M Y Y Y Y

Signed: Dated: D D M M Y Y Y Y

Continued overleaf

Part Eleven - Correspondence Address

Please state the address to which the correspondence should be sent if this is different to the address of Attorney One. State the full name and present address. If applicable, include the Company Name in Address Line 1

Mr ○ Mrs ○ Ms ○ Miss ○ Other ○

If Other, please specify here:

Last Name:

Forename 1:

Other Forenames:

Address 1:

Address 2:

Address 3:

Town/City:

County:

Postcode:

DX No. (solicitors only):

DX Exchange (solicitors only):

Attorney Date of Birth: D D M M Y Y Y Y

Occupation:

Daytime Tel No.:

Email Address:

Part Twelve - Additional Information

Please write down any additional information to support this application in the space below. If necessary attach additional paper to the end of this form.

Useful contacts

Part I Living wills

Books and leaflets

Advance Statements about Medical Treatment: Code of Practice with Explanatory Notes

By Ann Sommerville
British Medical Association, April 1995
ISBN 0727909142
£5.95

Withholding and withdrawing life-prolonging medical treatment; Guidance for decision-making

British Medical Association, 2nd edn, 2001
ISBN 0727916157
£9.95

Available from
BMJ Bookshop (the *British Medical Journal* is a BMA periodical)
Burton Street
London WC1H 9JR

Tel 020 7383 6244
Fax 020 7383 6455

Email orders@bmjbookshop.com
Or via the BMA website: www.bma.org.uk

Both titles are also available free on the internet at www.bmjpg.com

The New Natural Death Handbook

Edited by Nicholas Albery and Stephanie Wienrich of the Natural Death Centre
ISBN 0712605762
£10.99

Everything you always wanted to know about dying, from State benefits to green burials. A huge volume of information, not always very digestibly presented.

A Guide to Living Wills

The Voluntary Euthanasia Society
13 Prince of Wales Terrace
London W8 5PG

Tel 020 7376 7770
Fax 020 7376 2648

Email info@ves.org.uk
Website: www.ves.org.uk

Note that the VES states: 'The Voluntary Euthanasia Society does not provide help or advice on suicide.'

Organisations

British Medical Association

BMA House
Tavistock Square
London WC1H 9JP

General switchboard: Tel 020 7387 4499
Bookshop: 020 7383 6244
Medical Ethics Department: Tel 020 7383 6286; Fax 020 7383 6223

Email: ETHICS@bma.org.uk
Website: www.bma.org.uk

This website has a wealth of information about living wills. Try:
www.bma.org.uk/ap.nsf/Content/codeofpractice
www.bma.org.uk/ap.nsf/Content/consenttk2
www.bma.org.uk/ap.nsf/Content/advancestatements

In particular, you should read *End of Life Decisions – Views of the BMA*. It is important to understand the relationship between living wills and medical ethics. Go to www.bma.org.uk and type 'end of life decisions' in the search box.

Natural Death Centre

6 Blackstock Mews
Blackstock Road
London N4 2BT

Tel: 020 7359 839Fax: 020 7354 3831

www.naturaldeath.org.uk

Advice on living wills and many other death-related topics.

Terrence Higgins Trust

52-54 Grays Inn Road
London WC1X 8JU
Tel: 020 7831 0330
Fax: 020 7242 0121
Direct Helpline: 0845 1221200

Email: info@tht.org.uk
Website www.tht.org.uk

This registered charity offers advice on AIDS and HIV-related conditions and has produced a living will in conjunction with Kings College London.

Voluntary Euthanasia Society of London

13 Price of Wales Terrace
London W8 5PG

Tel: 020 7937 8721
Fax: 020 7376 2648

www.ves.org.uk

Information about voluntary euthanasia (see also under Books and Leaflets, above).

Alzheimer's Society

Gordon House
10 Greencoat Place
London SW1 1PH
Tel: 020 7306 0606

www.alzheimers.org.uk

Advice on living wills (including a draft living will) and many other age-related issues. The Society supports the use of living wills because 'they enable those with dementia to have a say in their future care'.

Age Concern England

Astral House
1268 London Road
London SW16 4ER

Tel: 0800 009 966

www.ageconcern.org.uk

Advice on living wills and many other age-related issues.

Age Concern Scotland

Tel: 0131 220 3345
www.ageconcernscotland.org.uk

Exit

17 Hart St
Edinburgh EH1 3RN

Tel: 0131 556 4404
Fax: 0131 557 4403

www.euthanasia.cc

Advice on end-of-life issues and living wills.

This site is promoted by Exit (formerly the Scottish Voluntary Euthanasia Society), and offers advice on living wills, notably the Living Will and Values History Project. They say, 'The Living Will and Values History Project was set up in response to an alarming growth and proliferation of living will documents that bore little correlation to academic and empirical data on their usefulness or effectiveness. It works no a non-profit basis and attempts to collate, analyse and apply research in this area, acting as an adviser and resource base, as well as publishing its own document'.

Exit's website includes a living will and a long list of books and articles on related subjects. Some do not apply to the UK, but even after weeding out such titles there is still a formidable choice of further reading.

First Do No Harm

This doctors' organisation takes its name from the Hippocratic oath and discusses recent end-of-life related issues (eg 'Miss B' – see p 8) from a pro-life point of view.

www.donoharm.org.uk

In surfing the web using the key word *euthanasia*, on which there are over a quarter of a million entries worldwide, you may also be directed towards the Church of Euthanasia website. One look at its motto – 'Suicide – abortion – cannibalism – sodomy' should be more than enough.

Religious considerations

Ebrahim Ahmed Jasat of the Muslim Burial Council of Leicestershire, which deals with death-related enquiries from all over the UK, kindly provided material on Muslim attitudes to death and living wills, including an Islamic Living Will. Contact him on 0116 273 0141.

You can find Anglican attitudes to life and death on the Church of England website: http://cofe.anglican.org.

Part 2 Enduring powers of attorney

Books and leaflets

Cretney and Lush on Enduring Powers of Attorney

By Denzil Lush
5th edn, published by Jordans, £45 – the professional's choice on this subject.

Enduring power of attorney – a guide to making an enduring power of attorney or taking on the role of attorney

Available from the PGO
Customer Services helpline: 0845 330 2900
www.guardianship.gov.uk and click on Enduring Power of Attorney.

Care home and nursing fees: Are you acting in the best interests of your clients?

By Pauline Thompson, Age Concern England
www.ageconcern.org.uk

Organisations

Public Guardianship Office

Archway Tower
2 Junction Road
London N19 5SZ

Customer services: 0845 330 2990
EPA helpline: 0845 330 2963
Complaints: 0845 330 2962
Accounts helpline: 0845 330 2962

Website: www.guardianship.gov.uk
Email: custserv@guardianship.gov.uk
Text phone: 020 7664 7755

In Scotland you can get more information about Continuing Attorneys and Welfare Attorneys from:

Office of the Public Guardian

Hadrian House
Callendar Business Park
Callendar Road
Falkirk
FK1 1XR

Tel: 01324 678 300
Fax: 01324 678301

www.publicguardian-scotland.gov.uk

The website gives access to various useful publications, including a layman's guide and a code of conduct.

The Scottish Executive has a website about the Adults with Incapacity (Scotland) Act 2000. The home page is at www.scotland.gov.uk/about/JD/CL/00016360/home.aspx

There is a useful leaflet about continuing attorneys and welfare attorneys at www.scotland.gov.uk/about/JD/CL/00016360/geninf.aspx

There is a superb factsheet called *Legal arrangements for managing financial affairs* which defines **mental capacity** and goes on to explain about agents, appointees and attorneys. You can download it from the Age Concern website:

www.ageconcern.org.uk/AgeConcern/media/Factsheet_22.pdf

Index

Notes

Notes

Notes

Notes

Notes

Notes

Notes

Notes

Notes

Notes

Notes